# Writers

### and Their

# Pets

Book design: Thomas Boucher
Illustration assistance: Yuri Meister

Library of Congress Cataloging-in-Publication Data available upon request.
ISBN: 978-1-947458-52-9

Duopress books are available at special discounts when purchased in bulk for sales
promotions as well as for fund-raising or educational use. Special editions can be
created to specification. Contact us at hello@duopressbooks.com for more information.

Manufactured in China
10 9 8 7 6 5 4 3 2 1

Duopress LLC
8 Market Place, Suite 300
Baltimore, MD 21202

Distributed by Workman Publishing Company, Inc.
Published simultaneously in Canada by Thomas Allen & Son Limited.

To order: hello@duopressbooks.com
www.duopressbooks.com
www.workman.com

# Writers
## and Their Pets

### True Stories of Famous Authors and Their Animal Friends

by
**Kathleen Krull**

art by
**Violet Lemay**

**dp**
duopress

# Contents

Introduction .................................................................. 6

Elizabeth Barrett Browning, *Her Immortal Dog* .................. 10

Edgar Allan Poe, *Scary and Strange* ............................... 18

Charles Dickens, *Keeper of the Raven* ............................. 28

Mark Twain, *Of Comedy and Cats* ................................. 36

Edith Wharton, *Writing Novels with a Lap Full of Dogs* ......... 46

Beatrix Potter, *Drawn to Mice and Bunnies* ....................... 50

Gertrude Stein, *A Poodle Is a Poodle Is a Poodle* ................ 60

Virginia Woolf, *A Dog of Her Own* ................................ 70

Dorothy Parker, *Devoted to Dogs* .................................. 78

William Faulkner, *Falling Off a Horse* ............................. 88

E. B. White, *Of Dogs, Pigs, and Spiders* ........................... 92

Ernest Hemingway, *A Soft Spot for Cats* ........................ 102

John Steinbeck, *The Famous Charley* ............................... 112

Marguerite Henry, *Queen of the Wild Ponies* ..................... 122

Pablo Neruda, *When Your Pet Saves Your Life* .................... 126

Kurt Vonnegut, *Black Humor with a Pumpkin Accent* ............. 136

Flannery O'Connor, *Life Is Better with Peacocks* ................. 140

Maurice Sendak, *Dogs and Other Wild Things* ..................... 148

Alice Walker, *Communing with Chickens* ............................ 158

J. K. Rowling, *The Best Reason to Have a Pet* ..................... 168

Glossary ............................................................... 178

More Books About These Great Writers ............................ 182

Citations ............................................................. 185

Index ................................................................. 188

# Introduction

The history of writers and their pets is long and charming.

Writing is a lonely craft, a battle to hold oneself aloof from the rest of the world in order to get words down on a page. Writers have to be solitary, avoiding ordinary distractions that could interfere with their extraordinary work.

But pets remind writers that they are *not* alone. Pets played one crucial role after another in the lives of the writers here.

Pets are unfailingly loyal, a solace during times of rejection from publishers, critics, and award committees. They watch us carefully, tuning in to our moods.

After a writer ventures into the unknown with flights of imagination, pets represent a safe harbor—companions who appreciate a writer's true self, no matter what mask he or she puts on for the public.

Pets indulge a writer's softer side. Mark Twain was a notorious lover of cuddly cats—but he was vastly outdone by Ernest Hemingway, who at one point had 57 of them! (He hailed them as "love sponges" and "purr factories.")

Pets can be—in the case of Maurice Sendak and several other writers here—better company than most people. For Elizabeth Barrett Browning, a dog provided such a source of security that she was able to function as a person and a poet.

Pets can be guardians, a role treasured by Virginia Woolf. Pets save lives emotionally—and in some cases, literally, as Pablo Neruda rejoiced.

Pets supply a way to unwind after hours of motionlessness, a way to get the blood flowing back to the head, which is what a writer wants. Charles Dickens loved this about his dogs, and William Faulkner rode his horses every day. They can be an aid to good health in all sorts of ways (except for the times horses threw Faulkner off). Grooming pets can be a soothing part of a daily routine, their breath ebbing and flowing with ours.

Pets excel at getting writers out of their own heads and relating to other people and the world. Writers have used pets to woo mates (E. B. White) and make friends out of strangers (John Steinbeck). Pets can make an ideal audience, sounding boards who never tire—unlike weary family and friends.

Pets brighten a writer's days, as her fabulous peafowl surely did for Flannery O'Connor. For some, playing silly games with a pet can make up for a bad childhood with no play and no pets.

Pets were muses to Gertrude Stein and many others. They can inspire an entire book—like Alice Walker and her irrepressible chickens. And as J. K. Rowling was tickled to find out, they can even help with the nightmare known as writer's block.

Attachments to pets can be so intense that many writers, like Dorothy Parker and Kurt Vonnegut, had their pets with them when they died. Sometimes pets died shortly after their owners, as with Edgar Allan Poe's Catterina.

Read on for more stories—amusing, touching, uplifting—of writers and their pets.

# Elizabeth Barrett Browning

—

*Her Immortal Dog*

"He and I are inseparable companions, and I have vowed him my perpetual society in exchange for his devotion." No, Elizabeth Barrett Browning wasn't writing about her future husband, the poet Robert Browning. She was referring to her dog.

Few were as attached to their pets as the enormously popular Victorian poet Elizabeth Barrett Browning. And few pets have made such a difference in a writer's life.

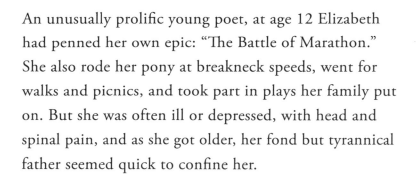

An unusually prolific young poet, at age 12 Elizabeth had penned her own epic: "The Battle of Marathon." She also rode her pony at breakneck speeds, went for walks and picnics, and took part in plays her family put on. But she was often ill or depressed, with head and spinal pain, and as she got older, her fond but tyrannical father seemed quick to confine her.

To this day, her ailment, or combination of them, remains a mystery. Whatever her illness, physical or mental, she became reclusive and anxious. Doctors did little for her except prescribe an opium/alcohol mixture, which may have worsened her symptoms. She spent most of her time in her upstairs room, always dressed in black, keeping caged doves, wasting away in foggy, dusty London.

Her health slowly improved as she headed into her thirties, though she wasn't writing and saw few people other than immediate family. Then, one day, a friend sent her a radiant, purebred cocker spaniel.

FLUSH

It was love at first sight. Flush (no one knows the story behind the name) was simply adorable. It didn't matter if he tore her letters, chewed her shoes, or wet her books. He made her laugh when he danced or played a game of climbing atop her head and tumbling down her shoulders. He woke her up each morning by gently nibbling her hands. They took coffee together, with him insisting on drinking out of a cup like hers, even though it made him sneeze. The maid bathed him and dried him with one of Elizabeth's shawls.

Elizabeth was afraid of many things, and loyal, joyful Flush made her feel safe, in that unique way that pets can soothe us—safe enough to resume contact with the outside world, through letters, and to begin writing poetry again.

Her work was experimental, sometimes shocking, and she wrote in every form—sonnets, ballads, epics, dramas, religious poems. She even wrote one of the great dog poems, "To Flush, My Dog," praising his glossy golden curls and irrepressible liveliness. Her influences included the English poet John Milton, the Italian poet Dante, and the feminist writer Mary Wollstonecraft.

Her first collection of poems revealed her passion for Greek politics. A later poem, "The Cry of the Children," condemned child labor and helped bring about child-labor reforms. Then, in 1844, her collection *Poems* brought her great success, attracting the admiration of poet Robert Browning, six years her junior: "I love your verses with all my heart, dear Miss Barrett," he began his letter.

Again, love at first sight—once Flush was appeased. He bit Robert, not once, but twice. Robert sensibly realized that Flush was just acting as dogs do and won him over with his favorite cakes.

(Flush had a sweet tooth and dined on macaroons, plum cake, and grapes.)

In one of literature's greatest love stories, Robert and Elizabeth's courtship had to be carried out in secret, for Elizabeth's father had forbidden any of his children to marry.

Wealthy London families at the time often had problems with dognappers, and poor Flush was dognapped three times and had to be ransomed. The third time, Elizabeth braved real danger to rescue him herself, paying the ransom though her father had said not to. She wrote to a friend, "I am so *flushified*, I can write of nothing else!" The adventure emboldened her to do what she did next.

One afternoon in 1846, carrying Flush, of course, Elizabeth met Robert at a bookstore. They made their way to the night ferry, which got them across the English Channel to France, and from there they traveled to the mild, sunny climate of Italy.

A plague of Italian fleas meant that Flush's golden curls

had to be shorn. But Browning blossomed. She ate in a restaurant for the first time and found happiness and health in Italy in all kinds of ways. Her father never forgave her for eloping, nor saw her again.

When she was 43 she had a son, whom they called Pen: "He doesn't talk yet much, but he gesticulates with extraordinary force of symbol, and makes surprising revelations to us every half-hour or so," she wrote. Flush was jealous at first but soon bonded with the boy, encouraged by Browning: "Flush loses nothing ... On the contrary, he is hugged and kissed (rather too hard sometimes), and never is permitted to be found fault with by anybody under the new regime. If Flush is scolded, Baby cries as matter of course."

And her writing flourished. This was the time of her most famous works, *Sonnets from the Portuguese* (which includes the classic "How Do I Love Thee?") and *Aurora Leigh*, about a strong and independent woman who embraces both work and love.

Among the many writers influenced by Browning was Edgar Allan Poe; she was one of the few contemporaries he liked. He borrowed the rhythm of one of her poems for "The Raven." After she praised it, Poe dedicated his collection *The Raven and Other Poems* to her, referring to her as "the noblest of her sex."

In her poems and in life she took stands against social injustice—not just child labor but slavery in the United States and injustice toward Italians by foreign rulers.

Flush died peacefully in 1854. Elizabeth Barrett Browning mourned but carried on. Seven years afterward, she too died, as Robert held her in his arms.

But Flush was not easily forgotten. Many years later, Virginia Woolf made him the narrator of her 1933 novel, *Flush: A Biography.* It was a witty romp about a dog's life, but also a biography of Browning and a chance to revisit favorite themes, like the need for oppressed women to find freedom.

In more ways than one, Flush had become immortal.

# Edgar Allan Poe

———

*Scary and Strange*

Edgar Allan Poe never smiled, even
with a beloved cat perched on his
shoulder. Despite his sad life, the
multitalented writer invented the
detective story *and* the horror story, as
well as helped develop science fiction.
He also wrote the only American poem
just about everybody knows.

By age two, Edgar Poe had lost both of his parents. In 1811, the tiny orphan was taken in by the Allan family. They never formally adopted him, and they didn't get along with him. All his life he mourned his lack of parental affection. Getting along with people was always going to be a problem for Poe.

Poe preferred the company of cats. "I wish I could write as mysterious as a cat," he once wrote admiringly.

After dropping out of college, having run up major gambling debts, Poe got himself expelled from the military academy at West Point. He took a job as an editor at a literary magazine in Richmond,

Virginia, which allowed him to try his hand at writing. His clever stories and gleefully harsh book reviews boosted the magazine's circulation several times over, and he only got fired twice in the process. As he moved on to a series of editorial positions at the leading magazines in Philadelphia and New York, he began spending his evenings writing his way to fame with scary, strange tales and poems.

Poe was the first well-known American writer to try to earn a living through writing alone. The result was a financially difficult life and career. Publishers routinely cheated writers, and writers plagiarized from each other without thinking twice. Plus Poe had a bad habit of antagonizing the very people who could have helped him. While working into the night on his gory tales, he supplemented his income with lectures and public readings. Often he was forced to beg friends and neighbors—the ones he hadn't alienated—for money.

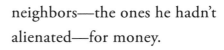

His short story "The Gold Bug" (starring a beetle) won a prize of $100 from a Philadelphia

newspaper, which increased his visibility. "The Raven" was a creepy poem of intense mourning: "Quoth the Raven 'Nevermore.'" It earned him only about $15 but made him internationally famous. Parodies of it popped up in newspapers, and kids followed him on the street, flapping their arms like scary black birds and chanting "nevermore." It became one of the best-known poems in American literature.

With "The Murders in the Rue Morgue" and other mysteries, he created the first modern detective stories. But he was drawn again and again to horror. His most frequent themes deal with death—its physical signs, the effects of decomposition, dread of being buried alive, the dead coming back to life, and the black misery of mourning. In his startling writing, the atmosphere is uniquely dark. Even the titles are scary: "The Fall of the House of Usher," "The Masque of the Red Death," "The Premature Burial," "The Imp of the Perverse,"

"The Tell-Tale Heart," "The Conqueror Worm," "The Haunted Palace," and "The Pit and the Pendulum" (in which rats are the heroes).

Many commented on Poe's unusually neat handwriting. He wrote on separate pieces of paper that he would attach together with sealing wax, then rolled it all up into a nice, tight scroll. As he recited a piece, he'd unfurl a scroll.

His work created a bizarre sensation and had enormous influence. It inspired everyone from Herman Melville to film director Alfred Hitchcock, from Jules Verne to Ray Bradbury and Stephen King. Poe was particularly respected in France.

Poe did not have a pet raven (that would be Charles Dickens, one of the only living writers Poe admired, whose raven is said to have inspired Poe's poem). With his awkward sense of humor, he would make a lame joke to visitors about his failure to keep ravens as pets. (Poe sometimes wrote jokes for money, but they weren't hilarious: Q. Why is a bleeding cat like a question? A. Because it's a category, or "catty gory.")

Poe did have cats. His first one was black, and it could perform the amazing feat of leaping up to the latch on the kitchen door with enough force to open it. Poe raved, "The writer of this article is the owner of one of the most remarkable black cats in the world—and this is saying much, for it will be remembered that black cats are all of them witches."

His most famous cat was a tabby with tortoiseshell markings named Catterina. They were devoted to each other. Whenever Poe had to travel, Catterina would go into a depression and stop eating. As Poe would sit down to write, the cat would climb up to his neck and then stay there, watching him work. She would remain on his shoulder the whole time. A visitor observed that she "purred as if in complacent approval of the world proceeding under [her] supervision."

Catterina

But Poe could turn anything into a nightmare, even a pet, and he once wrote a horror story called "The Black Cat," in which the cat meets a nasty end.

Poe married his very young cousin Virginia. He called her Sissy, perhaps because their relationship was more like brother and sister than husband and wife. He often read his poems aloud to Sissy and could make himself cry at his own words. She was sickly, but he was drawn to sickliness, and her illness inspired much of his work. When she began coughing up blood, it was plain to see she was dying of tuberculosis, the then-fatal lung disease. Poe was in denial and never stopped believing she'd recover.

They had few possessions—just the cat, tropical birds he kept in cages, books, and two pine tables he had built. They lived in rented rooms in boardinghouses. Sometimes they were so poor they lived on bread and molasses for weeks.

As Sissy lay dying on a straw bed in their unheated room, Poe placed his old military coat on her for warmth, to which Catterina added by sleeping on top of her. She died, still only 24. Poe plunged into deep mourning, but flailing about in his grief, he also began wooing assorted other women with poetry.

Two years later, Poe was found in a Baltimore bar, dead at age 40. It's never been clear whether his death was from drinking—he did have an unhealthy relationship with alcohol—or heart failure or some other cause. Scholars have proposed dozens of theories about Poe's mysterious death.

In any case, Catterina was distraught. Two weeks after Poe's death, she was also found dead.

Poe's influence even reached to football: The Baltimore Ravens are named for his famous menacing **bird**. The team's mascot is named "Poe," who was joined by two other mascots, "Edgar" and "Allan," until they were retired in 2008.

# Charles Dickens

—

Keeper of the Raven

One of most important and
influential writers in history, this
English author wrote 15 novels (10 of
them longer than 800 pages), while
devoting himself to pets, especially
his raven, Grip the Knowing.

Charles Dickens had no time or money for pets during his tough childhood. As his father went to prison for debt, 12-year-old Dickens was taken out of school. He had to go to work in a factory, pasting labels on shoe polish. Images of prison and of oppressed or traumatized children recur in many of his novels.

When his father was released, Dickens's unsupportive mother wanted her son to keep working. But he was able to manage just a year or two more of school. He wrote short stories and sold them to classmates for marbles.

He worked his way up to becoming a newspaper reporter, then began contributing stories and essays to magazines. When he wrote the first installment of *The Pickwick Papers,* it was all the rage, and Dickens became the most popular author of the day at age 24. Dickens soared on to such masterpieces as *Oliver Twist* (the first novel ever with a child as its hero), *Nicholas Nickleby, David Copperfield* (his own favorite of his books), *Bleak House, A Tale of Two Cities,* and *Great Expectations.* His works came out in the installment format, which allowed him to evaluate reactions, and he often changed his plot and characters based on such feedback.

Those who celebrate Christmas have Dickens to thank for much of the Christmas spirit. His novel *A Christmas Carol* influenced the way the holiday was celebrated, morphing it from a day on the religious calendar to a vast family-centered festival of generosity. The greeting "Merry Christmas" comes from the book, as does "Bah! Humbug!" as uttered by the awful miser Ebenezer Scrooge.

Dickens had a thrilling way with cliffhanger endings to each installment, keeping readers in high suspense. Even people who couldn't read came up with pennies to have each new monthly episode read to them, creating a whole new tradition of popular literature.

Readers loved his immensely colorful people—Dickens created some of the world's best-known fictional characters—as well as his sense of humor and his strong plots. The term "Dickensian" came to describe work featuring miserable social conditions or comically repulsive characters.

His books were so easy to adapt for the stage that sometimes twenty London theaters would produce simultaneous adaptations of his latest story—again, allowing nonreaders to applaud his writing.

A magnificent performer himself, Dickens was drawn to the theater and had nearly become a professional actor when young. He found he could earn more by reading than by writing, and he toured energetically with spellbinding renditions of his works. He was very much a public figure, the best speaker of the age, similar to Mark Twain, who acknowledged Dickens as the pioneer.

Dickens enjoyed a wider popularity during his lifetime than had any previous writer, and he moved to a three-story estate. He had married Catherine Hogarth, settling down and raising their nine children. He called her "Mouse" and "Dearest Pig" when they were getting along, and "Donkey" when they weren't. Eventually he left Catherine for an actress 27 years his junior, whom he lived with until his death.

An all-out animal person once he grew up and could afford them, Dickens had dogs, a canary, a pony, an eagle, and plenty of cats. His favorite pet was a raven he called Grip the Knowing. It bit the children's and servants' ankles, but Dickens admired its talkative ways. Grip learned to mimic speech, and Dickens lovingly recorded the bird's vocabulary,

GRIP

*"Halloa, old girl!"*

being his favorite expression.

Grip the Knowing even played a role in literary history. He appeared in Dickens's novel *Barnaby Rudge*, which was well reviewed by Edgar Allen Poe. Poe was then inspired to pen his legendary poem "The Raven," all about the bird's ominous and prophetic utterings.

Alas, a few months after swallowing a white paint chip, Grip perished. Dickens wrote of the bird's final moments in extravagant, silly detail: "He was heard talking to himself about the horse and [the coachman's] family, and to add some incoherent expressions which are supposed to have been either a foreboding of his approaching dissolution or some wishes relative to the disposal of his little property, consisting chiefly of half-pence which he has buried in different parts of the garden. On the clock striking twelve he appeared slightly agitated, but he soon recovered, walked twice or thrice along the coachhouse, stopped to bark, staggered, exclaimed 'Halloa old girl!'...and died."

After Grip died, Dickens had him professionally embalmed and mounted. He replaced the pet with other ravens, like Grip the Clever and Grip the Wicked.

Dickens wrote neatly with a goose-quill pen in blue ink on blue-gray paper. He insisted on total quiet and had an extra door installed to his study to block out noise. He worked the same long hours every day, and if the words weren't coming he doodled or stared out the window.

Pets provided relief. He made it a point to walk the streets, his dogs trotting behind him, for exactly the amount of time as he sat writing. He walked fast—he was once clocked at 4.8 miles per hour—and gained an encyclopedic knowledge of London.

He spent the last ten years of his life in the company of a deaf kitten, letting the cat sit with him as he wrote. Exhausted from touring, he died suddenly after a stroke.

In English literature, he is considered second only to William Shakespeare.

"What greater gift than the love of a cat?" Dickens once asked. Cats who needed his attention knew how to extinguish the flame on his desk candle. When his favorite, **Bob**, died, he was so upset that he had Bob's paw stuffed and mounted to an ivory letter opener, engraved "In memory of Bob, 1862."

# Mark Twain

—

## Of Comedy
## and Cats

"When a man loves cats, I am his friend and comrade, without further introduction," said Mark Twain, a beloved figure in American literature. He was a novelist, humorist, popular entertainer, political philosopher, and travel writer.

Mark Twain's life was full of mishaps and outright tragedy. He met his misfortunes with verve and as much humor as he could muster. It turned out that he could pour his woes into comic writing. His motto was:

*"Against the assault of laughter nothing can stand."*

Humor was sort of a weapon—it galvanized him to get through tough times and made him feel less alone.

So did cats, of which he had lots as soon as he could afford them.

It wasn't until he was in his thirties that Twain started establishing himself with his funny writing. Before

this, he had tried a great many things, having gone to
work at age 15. He started off doing odd jobs around
Hannibal, Missouri, always carrying a book with him.
Restless and ambitious, he traveled widely. His favorite
of his apprenticeships was to the captain of a steamboat
on the Mississippi River. Riverboat pilot seemed like
the ideal job. (Born Samuel Clemens, he took the
pseudonym "Mark Twain" from a steamboating term.)
The pay was good, the job earned respect, and a pilot
was free and self-sufficient.

Could these perks also apply to writing? He worked
his way up from printer's apprentice to contributing
sketches and articles to his brother's paper, writing
letters to a newspaper, and getting a job as a reporter—
then came a brainstorm about a frog.

Twain didn't have an athletic frog, but his
amusing breakthrough story starred one:
"The Celebrated Jumping Frog of Calaveras
County." He discovered he had a "'call' to

literature of a low order"—humorous writing—"it is nothing to be proud of, but it is my strongest suit." Humorous literature was a new thing to Americans and not widely considered respectable.

His first book was in fact *The Celebrated Jumping Frog of Calaveras County and Other Sketches.* It did not sell well. A book about his experiences in the West—*Roughing It*—did a little better.

On his first date with Olivia Langdon, he took her to see Charles Dickens, famous author and marvelous speaker. When Langdon's father wanted to check into his background—jumping around from job to job, from state to state—the reports were all negative. Twain persisted in his courtship, eventually winning all the Langdons over.

Making Twain famous were his stories of boys growing up along the Mississippi River. First was *The Adventures of Tom Sawyer*, about the humorous antics of Tom and his comrades. Twain treated childhood in a new way, not depicting kids falling in line with adult authority, but as a time of mischief, fun, and affection.

Huck Finn had appeared in *Tom Sawyer*, and Twain decided that the unschooled runaway (from his abusive father) deserved his own story. *Adventures of Huckleberry Finn* deals with Huck's struggle helping the runaway slave Jim while also escaping from the unwanted influences of so-called civilization.

Missouri was a slave state when Twain had grown up there. *Huckleberry Finn*, addressing the shameful legacy of slavery, has generated debate from those who found the book patronizing toward African Americans. But Twain hated slavery, was disgusted by racism, and paid the expenses of the first black students at various colleges.

Getting wealthy with his writing, he moved his family to a farm in Hartford, Connecticut. It had nineteen luxurious rooms and five bathrooms. He spent summers on a farm near Elmira, New York. There he typed his stories (he was the first professional writer to use a typewriter) in a small eight-sided room lined with windows. Family members would blow a horn if they needed him.

Twain got his three daughters three collies, naming them I Know, You Know, and Don't Know. But mainly he was a sucker for cats: "I simply can't resist a cat, particularly a purring one. They are the cleanest, cunningest, and most intelligent things I know." He often said that animals were in many ways superior to the human race.

Twain kept as many as 11 cats at a time. He carried them around on his shoulders and gave them personalities.

After his daughter Clara had to be hospitalized, she smuggled a kitten into her room and named it Bambino. A patient allergic to cats complained, and she gave it to her father. Twain doted on Bambino and was distraught when it disappeared one day. He promptly took out an ad in the newspaper, offering a reward for Bambino's safe return: "Large and intensely black; thick, velvety fur; has a faint fringe of white hair across his chest; not easy to find in ordinary light."

BAMBINO

**MARK TWAIN HAS LOST A BLACK CAT.**

Have you seen a distinguished looking cat that looks as if it might be lost? If you have take it to Mark Twain, for it may be his. The following advertisement was received at the American office Saturday night:

**A CAST LOST - FIVE DOLLARS REWARD** for his restoration to Mark Twain, No. 21 Fifth avenue. Large and intensely black; thick, velvety fur; has a faint fringe of white hair across his chest; not easy to find in ordinary light.

A steady stream of people bearing cats showed up at Twain's door. They came even after Bambino was found meowing across the street. It was a case of people doing anything to get a glimpse of the funniest man in America, someone who was actually helping to shape it.

Even as he succeeded with *A Connecticut Yankee in King Arthur's Court*, *The Prince and the Pauper*, and *Life on the Mississippi*, Twain was getting deeper in debt, thanks to terrible judgment in investments. He was able to pay his creditors in full by launching a brilliant speaking career—with standing ovations from his very first appearance. Dressed in his famous white three-

Twain favored whimsical names for his cats—**Lazy**, **Satan**, **Sin**, **Cleveland**, **Pestilence**, **Famine**, and **Sour Mash**—and names that were tongue twisters, supposedly to help his children learn pronunciation— **Apollinaris** (who always wore bows), **Zoroaster**, **Blatherskite**, and **Beelzebub**.

*Apollinaris*

piece linen suit—
which made him
feel "clean in a dirty
world"—he had
audiences howling
with laughter.

Two of his adored
daughters died before
him, as did his beloved
wife. He kept writing,
he said, "to keep my
heart from breaking."
A heart attack was
what eventually killed him, in 1910.

Later writers cherished him. Said Ernest Hemingway, "All
modern American literature comes from one book by Mark
Twain called *Huckleberry Finn*." The "father of American
literature" was what William Faulkner called him.

# Edith Wharton

—

## Writing Novels with
a Lap Full of Dogs

The brilliant American writer Edith Wharton was born Edith Jones in 1862. Her distinguished New York family, with its pampered pets, was so fancy that the saying "keeping up with the Joneses" (living up to the high standards of the neighbors) is said to refer to it.

Her love of dogs started at age four, when her father gave her a spitz called Foxy, a dog who, she said later, made her feel human for the first time. Two years later, she began walking around the living room reciting stories she had written. Her mother frowned, as she believed Edith's job was simply to marry well. But Edith kept writing anyway—short stories, her first novel at age 11, a book of poems at 16.

At 17, she made her debut in high society, and a few years later she married Edward Wharton, a wealthy banker. Her marriage was lonely, as Edward suffered from serious mental illness. She divorced him after 28 years of marriage.

She found companionship with countless lapdogs—Chihuahuas, Pekingese, and poodles. She hired a "dog-knitter" to make them sweaters, played silly games with them, gave them jeweled collars, let them drape her shoulders, and once wrote this love poem: "My little old dog:/A heart-beat/At my feet."

Wharton designed The Mount, her dream home in Lenox, Massachusetts. She published more than 50 acclaimed books—including *The House of Mirth*, *Ethan Frome*, and *The Age of Innocence*, which made her the first woman to win the Pulitzer Prize for Literature.

The Mount featured a pet cemetery with stones marking the graves of Mimi, Toto, Miza, and Jules, four of her dogs. She could see the cemetery as she wrote, surrounded by her living dogs, gazing out at her dead ones.

# Beatrix Potter

---

*Drawn to Mice
and Bunnies*

An English writer, artist, pet lover, natural scientist, and conservationist, Beatrix Potter was best known for *The Tale of Peter Rabbit* and other charming children's books featuring animals.

Except for her brother Bertram, Beatrix Potter grew up isolated from other children. The family was extremely wealthy, and she was homeschooled by private tutors. She remained friends with one of them, Annie, for many years afterward.

Yet Beatrix and Bertram were not lonely. They had numerous small animals as pets—not just for fun, but to observe closely and draw endlessly. In their schoolroom, Beatrix and Bertram kept mice, rabbits, a hedgehog, and even bats, along with collections of butterflies and other insects that they drew and studied.

Spot

Beatrix was devoted to her animals, always catching and taming mice. One of her mice loved to have fights with her handkerchief but chewed a hole in her sheets and found other ways to get in trouble with the grown-ups. She had pet rabbits named Benjamin Bouncer and Peter Piper and drew them from every possible angle. Her days were filled with caring for a brilliant green lizard named Judy, a whole family of snails named the Bill family, a pet dormouse named Xarifa, a green frog named Punch, and a more typical pet, a spaniel named Spot.

Beatrix spent holidays either in Scotland or the scenic English Lake District. This further inspired her love of landscape, flora, and fauna, all of which she closely observed and painted. Her first sketchbook studied a dozen caterpillars in great detail. By eight she was drawing animals with clothes, wearing ice skates, jackets, hats.

At 14, Potter began to keep a diary. Writing in code that she devised, she reported in tiny handwriting on life in general, her impressions of art and artists, and books she read on her path as a self-taught artist and writer. She loved fairy tales and fantasy. She grew up with *Aesop's Fables*, the fairy tales of the Brothers Grimm and Hans Christian Andersen, Charles Kingsley's *The Water Babies*, and Shakespeare. She adored Edward Lear's *Book of Nonsense*, which included the beloved "The Owl and the Pussycat," and Lewis Carroll's *Alice in Wonderland*. The Brer Rabbit stories of Joel Chandler Harris were also favorites.

In art, she was influenced by the work of Walter Crane, Kate Greenaway, and especially Randolph Caldecott, an artist whose work was collected by her father. When she first started to illustrate stories, she focused on traditional rhymes and stories, like "Cinderella," "Sleeping Beauty," "Ali Baba and the Forty Thieves," and "Red Riding Hood."

As a way to earn their own money when they were young, Beatrix and her brother, Bertram, began to design and print cards for Christmas and other occasions. The most frequent subjects? **Mice** and **rabbits**.

But most often her illustrations veered toward fantasies featuring her own pets: mice, rabbits, kittens, and guinea pigs.

Potter's former teacher Annie and her eight children were the lucky recipients of many of Potter's first stories. She put them into letters full of delightful pictures. Still taking her holidays in Scotland at age 27, one day she sent an illustrated animal story to cheer up Noel, Annie's sick son. She used the name of her own pet rabbit at the time, Peter, whom she had trained to do tricks, and based him on her close observations. She devised adventures for Peter and gave him a mother and three sibling bunnies named Flopsy, Mopsy, and Cottontail.

Peter was full of personality, a naughty one, and far more adventurous than his siblings. No sooner had their mother told them to avoid Mr. McGregor's garden while she was out shopping—their father had had an unfortunate "accident" there and ended up being baked into a pie—than the little rabbit disobeyed. He squeezed himself under the garden gate to chomp on the forbidden vegetables. Making a narrow escape from Mr. McGregor, he was sent straight to bed by his mother with chamomile tea.

It was Annie who gave Beatrix the idea to publish the story.

Six publishers promptly rejected it. So Potter decided to self-publish it as *The Tale of Peter Rabbit* in 1901. The next year a publisher picked it up, and it became one of the

best-selling children's books of all time. It was a brand-new form of animal fable, combining scientific accuracy with fanciful behavior. The animals were not just adorable and cute, but models of anatomical accuracy.

Her publisher was thrilled to discover that their new author had an endless supply of ideas. She dreamed up stories, rhymes, and animal characters—Jeremy Fisher, Jemima Puddle-Duck, Mrs. Tiggy-Winkle, and many more. Potter went on to create dozens of books, from *The Tailor of Gloucester* to *The Tale of Squirrel Nutkin* and *The Tale of Benjamin Bunny*. The books combined deceptively simple prose, dry humor, and detailed watercolor illustrations. They were tiny so that even the smallest children could hold them.

Potter kept researching, sometimes going to extreme lengths. She captured two wild mice—which she named Hunca Munca and Tom Thumb—and other rodents and kept them in beautiful Victorian cages on her drawing table. After sketching their shiny fur and bright eyes, she went on to dissect the animals to study their muscle structure. Potter's illustrations might have been cute, but they were also realistic in every detail.

Tom Thumb

Hunca Munca

She also had more traditional pets: two Pekingese dogs named Tzusee and Chuleh. She adored them and used them as foot warmers in bed.

At age 39, with six popular books to her credit, she spent much of her time with her pets at Hill Top, a small farm in the Lake District. She bought it with some money left to her and the royalties from her books. She eventually married her lawyer and spent the last 30 years of her life breeding prize-winning sheep.

She kept extending her property by buying additional farms, wanting to protect the unique hill country landscape. She is credited with preserving much of the land that now makes up the Lake District National Park.

Potter continued to write and draw, although mostly for her own pleasure. She was a generous patron of the Girl Guides, whose troops she allowed to make their summer camps on her land.

At her death in 1943, she was the owner of 16 farms full of animals.

# Gertrude Stein

—

## A Poodle Is a Poodle Is a Poodle

Gertrude Stein was a keeper of poodles named Basket and an influential American experimental writer who was not commercially successful until age 59, with *The Autobiography of Alice B. Toklas*, which was actually her own life story.

Gertrude Stein's first pet was a canary named Dick. Growing up around Oakland and San Francisco, California, books were more important to her than pets. She spent all of her allowance at secondhand bookstores. Brainy and bold, she graduated from Radcliffe College with high honors and went on to medical school.

While studying to become a doctor, she wrote on the top of one exam that she wasn't in the mood to take a test. The professor still gave her the top mark. But she dropped out just short of earning her medical degree—bored with her studies, upset at the discrimination against women doctors, and more and more interested in writing.

In her twenties Stein left America for good with her brother Leo and settled in Paris, becoming a novelist, poet, playwright, savvy art collector, and major influence on others. At first she was famous for her art collection, buying works by Pablo Picasso, Paul Cézanne, Henri Matisse, and others long before they were popular.

Her lifetime partner, Alice B. Toklas—the two women married in Italy in 1910—ran their household while Stein devoted herself to writing. She worshipped the novelists Henry James and George Eliot, but she wanted to break new ground. Her self-confidence was extraordinary:

ALICE · GERTRUDE

"I am a genius…In my generation I am the only one," she said. She also called herself "the creative literary mind of the century."

With her prose, she crafted experiments in which it was often hard to find the meaning—and then she experimented with her experiments. Liberating language from its normal rules, she used words that were not even words and believed that commas were a sign of weakness. Her work was fragmented and repetitious, with slight variations.

Some of Stein's lines became immortal, like "Rose is a rose is a rose is a rose." She said of Oakland, "there is no there there." On her deathbed she asked, "What is the question?"

Was it nonsense or genius? Even her beloved brother called it "rubbish." (Soon afterward, they stopped speaking.)

Picasso knew how very fond of **pigs** Stein was, and he always brought her his pig drawings.

A multitasker, Stein wrote *during* errands as Toklas drove the couple around in their Model T Ford, which they called Aunt Pauline. (The car was named after Stein's real aunt because the car, like the aunt, "always behaved admirably in emergencies and behaved fairly well most of the time if she was properly flattered.") When Toklas dashed into stores, Stein would perch in the driver's seat, pull out a pencil and a scrap of paper, and let her mind wander. She was particularly inspired by traffic on the busy Parisian streets. Cars stopped and started with a rhythm that morphed into words.

She herself learned how to drive in order to deliver emergency supplies during World War I, but her driving was scary. She disliked maps and never mastered driving in reverse—she'd simply find a way to her destination by moving forward.

She wrote only about half an hour every day. The

dazzling social life of their salon filled the rest of her days. With a contagious laugh, she asked nosy questions as she poured coffee and Toklas passed around pastries. She hosted Ernest Hemingway, F. Scott Fitzgerald, Richard Wright, and just about every contemporary writer of note. Doing all she could to foster their talents, she was especially influential on Hemingway: "Gertrude Stein and me are just like brothers," he bragged. She'd hurry to bed before dawn so the chirping birds wouldn't keep her awake.

Dogs were crucial to the Stein/Toklas household. They had two Chihuahuas, named Byron and Pépé, and a hound called Polpe, who loved to smell flowers.

Ever since reading Henry James's *The Princess Casamassima*, Toklas had always wanted a white poodle. Her dream came true one day when they were out in the country and found a little poodle puppy in a neighborhood dog show. The puppy jumped up into

Stein's arms. Toklas named him Basket—she thought he looked so stylish that he should carry a basket of flowers in his mouth (something he never actually accomplished).

But he did inspire Stein's writing. Even as he grew large and unwieldy, he would jump into Stein's lap and stay there. She claimed that listening to the rhythm of him drinking water made her recognize the difference between sentences and paragraphs, that paragraphs are emotional and sentences are not.

Basket appeared in her work: "I am I because my little dog knows me, even if the little dog is a big one."

When Basket died, he was succeeded by other white

poodles, Basket I and later Basket II. It was part of Stein and Toklas's routine to brush the current Basket's teeth each morning. He had his own toothbrush, of course. He would be bathed in sulfur water each day, and then Stein would make her guests run the dog in circles around the yard until he was dry.

BASKET I

BASKET II

The dogs became famous, photographed by the most illustrious photographers of the day.

Fortunately, Basket II was a pedigreed purebred dog, so he survived the German occupation of France during World War II—Nazis forbade the feeding of all pets

except those with pedigrees. Both Jewish, Stein and Toklas fled Paris to the countryside to keep under the radar of Nazis, befriending many young American servicemen who visited them.

So skilled did they become at pet care that on the final page of *The Autobiography of Alice B. Toklas,* Stein included her role as "pretty good vet for dogs." The book, which was actually her own life story wittily told from Alice's point of view, was a sudden bestseller. Other books were not—like her first novel, *Q.E.D.,* which she never even tried to publish. She self-published *Three Lives* and later wrote another novel, *The Making of Americans,* and the words for an opera, *Four Saints in Three Acts.* She finished *The Mother of Us All* (an opera about Susan B. Anthony) just before her death in 1946.

The last Basket was of great comfort to Toklas after Stein's death—until he, too, died: "For some time," Toklas wrote afterward, "I have realized how much I depended upon him and so it is the beginning of living for the rest of my days without anyone who is dependent upon me for anything."

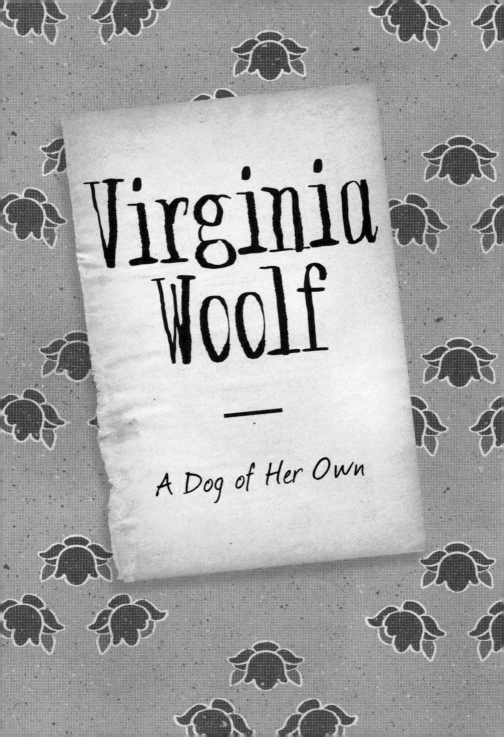

# Virginia Woolf

—

*A Dog of Her Own*

"A woman must have money and a room of her own to write fiction," English writer Virginia Woolf famously declared. And a dog, she might well have added.

Dogs were a significant part—the fun part—of Virginia Woolf's often dark life. She once wrote: "This you'll call sentimental—perhaps—but then a dog somehow represents—no I can't think of the word—the private side of life—the play side."

Shag

Woolf's first published essay, for a religious newspaper, was an obituary for Shag, the beloved family pet. After he was hit by a car, she wrote "On a Faithful Friend." She had relied on the mutt for companionship as she suffered through a series of tragic family deaths. He was also a way for her to hang out with Vanessa, her adored sister who was technically Shag's owner.

The next dog was Gurth, a sheepdog trained to look after sheep. Now, at all times, he looked after Woolf, who was often depressed and ill. He brought her out of herself and allowed her to take care of another being. She took him everywhere—the library, concerts (except when he howled, then she had to get him

Gurth

outside), exploring London neighborhoods: "Gurth wears my life out," she pretended to protest.

By this time Virginia, Vanessa, and their two brothers had moved to the free-spirited Bloomsbury section of London. They formed the fabled Bloomsbury Group, gloriously free to pursue studies, paint or write, and entertain. There Virginia met Leonard Woolf, whom she eventually married.

Was she attracted to him because of his last name? In any case, Leonard became her protector, almost Gurth-like, and her writing career began in earnest.

She was best known for her serious novels, especially *Mrs. Dalloway* and *To the Lighthouse,* as well as the playful *Orlando: A Biography*. Her style was experimental, pioneering in stream-of-consciousness storytelling. Her stories didn't necessarily unfold in a linear way but were told by way of what the characters were thinking. Woolf also wrote influential essays, diaries, and nonfiction. In *A Room of One's Own*, she attributed women's absence from history not on a lack of brains and talent but on their lack of money.

Woolf took an animal detour when she received her first check for her writing: "I have to admit that instead of spending that sum upon bread and butter, rent, shoes and stockings, or butcher's bills, I went out and **bought a cat**—a beautiful cat, a fluffy Persian cat."

To work around the notorious difficulty of getting published, she and Leonard founded their own publishing company, Hogarth Press. It wasn't just for self-publishing—they also brought out works by Sigmund Freud, Katherine Mansfield, T. S. Eliot, E. M. Forster, and others.

Virginia wrote standing up, not for health reasons but because of sibling rivalry. Her sister Vanessa, a prominent painter, painted while standing, and Virginia didn't want to be outdone. She used different-colored inks in her pens—greens, blues, and purples (her favorite).

She and Leonard always had dogs. One of their few disagreements was that she liked them wild and he liked them well-behaved.

Probably most important was Pinka, a purebred black cocker spaniel. Even though Pinka chewed holes in Woolf's skirts, ate manuscripts, and interrupted their nightly games of lawn bowling when she dashed after a ball, Woolf saw her as "an angel of light." Leonard adored her, even "after she has wetted his floor eight times in one day," and he allowed Pinka to lick his nose as he worked (not like him at all). The dog kept Woolf company in her small writing hut and on the long walks she took to help her unwind. Pinka helped her look around and be aware of nature, like the change of seasons, and listened as she talked through long sections of her writing while walking.

*Pinka*

Sometimes Woolf was too ill to write, and dogs helped her endure the empty hours: "Half the horrors of illness cease when one has a book or a dog or a cup of one's own at hand."

While reading the love letters of Elizabeth Barrett and Robert Browning, with their mention of the beloved spaniel Flush, Woolf was intrigued. She found that "the figure of their dog made me laugh so I couldn't resist making him a Life." Using Pinka's antics as a model, she wrote *Flush: A Biography,* a book told from a dog's point of view. It was a joke, a spree. But she spent two years on it, all the while worrying that if it was popular, her serious work could be dismissed. In fact, it became her bestselling book to date and a Book of the Month Club selection in America.

But over time it failed to eclipse her other works. Many writers claim her as an influence—Margaret Atwood, Gabriel García Márquez, Toni Morrison. A large body of literature is dedicated to her life and work, and she has been the subject of many plays, novels, and films.

One day the Woolfs came back from a trip to find Pinka unexpectedly dead, a terrible blow.

A month after Pinka's death they bought a black and

white purebred spaniel they named Sally. But Woolf never bonded with her in the same way and thought of her as Leonard's dog.

Adding to her grief over Pinka was the looming horror of World War II. Woolf worried that all writing was simply irrelevant when it seemed England was on the verge of invasion and civilization was about to end. More and more, she found herself paralyzed by depression. On March 28, 1941, she walked behind their house down to the River Ouse, put stones in her pockets, and drowned herself. There was no dog accompanying her when she died.

Scholars have debated about her illness and usually give a diagnosis of bipolar disorder, which would have been treatable today. There was no effective treatment in her lifetime, just the careful nursing of Leonard—and the company of dogs.

Sally

# Dorothy Parker

___

Devoted to Dogs

One of the great literary humorists,
the Queen of Snark, Dorothy Parker
was also famous for never being without a pet dog.

RAGS

By her own admission, Dorothy Parker was "a plain, disagreeable child with stringy hair and a yen to write poetry." Her first dog was Rags, a beloved Boston terrier whom she spoiled rotten, writing him loving letters when they were apart.

Parker was working as a pianist at a dance school when she fell into writing light verse. Her break came when she sold a poem, "Any Porch," to *Vanity Fair*. She soon became the magazine's drama critic, with a sparkling wit and a low opinion of just about everything. She was eventually let go after one too many mean reviews and went flying into a solo career.

She published some 300 poems in various magazines, and in 1926, her first volume of poetry became a bestseller with great reviews. She also contributed short stories to the *New Yorker*. All but single-handedly, she set the tone considered typical for *New Yorker* short stories—a spare, sophisticated, melancholy tale, later associated with J. D. Salinger and John Cheever. She also became the magazine's book reviewer, known as "Constant Reader."

Many of her heroines were strong characters facing difficulties all too familiar to 21st-century women. In 1929 Parker won the O. Henry Award for the best short story of the year with "Big Blonde."

She was such an obsessive reviser that she once lamented, "I can't write five words but that I change seven."

During this time she was one of the founding members of the ultimate in-group, the Algonquin Round Table. This was a literary lunch that lasted for years, gathering at Manhattan's Algonquin Hotel around a round table in the center of the dining room. Parker sometimes lived at the hotel, so all she had to do was take the elevator down to lunch every day. She was perhaps the most famous member—less than five feet tall, but with a killer wit she wielded like a razor-sharp knife.

WOODROW WILSON

Parker always carried a dog. Early on she got a Boston terrier that reminded her of Rags. She patriotically named him Woodrow Wilson, and when he died it took her a long time to get over it. Eventually she accepted an Airedale puppy as a gift. He had a habit of chewing the furniture at the Algonquin, eating sofas and armchairs, until she finally had to give him to friends in the country.

She couldn't stand rats but otherwise loved all animals. When fishing, she threw back everything she caught, too worried about the poor fish's families.

She was attracted to stray dogs on the street (horses as well, but they would have been much harder to smuggle into her hotel room). Once, she rescued a stray after a late night on Sixth Avenue. She took the dog home, cleaned it up, and presented it to wealthy friends, tickled by the thought of the mutt living a posh lifestyle.

Most unusually, she adopted an alligator she found in a taxi and housed it in her bath-tub, until her maid quit with a note, perhaps embellished by Parker: "I cannot work in a house with alliga-tors. I would have told you this before, but I never thought the subject would come up."

Parker never bothered to housebreak her dogs and would forget to take them

FRAULEIN

SCRAMBLES

out, secretly amused when they peed in fashionable homes. This wasn't usually a big deal in New York, but in Beverly Hills, California, it was different. If she brought Fraulein, a dachshund, and Scrambles, a mutt, into fancy hotels, she was met with disapproval. When one hotel manager scolded her for her dog's "accident," she declared "I did it" and stormed out.

She had come to Hollywood as a film writer. She received screen credits for more than 15 films, including *A Star Is Born*, one of two movies for which she was nominated for an Academy Award.

Parker is easily the most-quoted woman in dictionaries of quotations. When told that the famously silent former president Calvin Coolidge had died, she was said to have asked, "How can they tell?" Of actress

Katharine Hepburn's performance in a play, Parker said she "ran the gamut of emotions from A to B." Her ferocious response as Constant Reader to the whimsical A. A. Milne's *The House at Pooh Corner*: "Tonstant Weader fwowed up."

Parker truly believed there was no such thing as too many dogs. In London she bought Timothy, a Dandie Dinmont terrier who fought with every single animal he encountered. Then Robinson came into Parker's realm, a dachshund who liked to sleep curled up under her chair. He was attacked by a larger dog and, to her sorrow, died.

TIMOTHY

ROBINSON

On a trip to France, Parker bought a Scottish terrier, Daisy, of whose intelligence she was wildly proud: "Why, that dog is practically a Phi Beta Kappa," she wrote. "She can sit up and beg, and she can give her paw—I don't say she will but she can."

DAISY

Next was Wolf, a Bedlington terrier, who of course required a friend, Cora, another Bedlington terrier. Then she had Flic, a boxer who was scared of everything. Once, Norman Mailer's ferocious German shepherd attacked Flic and had to be pulled off. In the melee a finger got bit, and Parker wouldn't see Mailer again for nine years. Then she was on to Misty, a silver poodle, then Cliché, another poodle.

In her writing she could direct her sparkling wit at dogs: "No woman who owns that lily of the field, a Pekingese, can be accused of selfishness," she wrote. "She simply hasn't the time to think of herself. His Serene Highness demands unceasing attention."

When she wrote "Verse for a Certain Dog," she started on a sentimental note: "Such glorious faith as fills your limpid eyes, / Dear little friend of mine, I never knew." But amid the compliments, she scolds—about the pup chewing her shoe, eating dirty bones in the house, getting too close to the goldfish bowl, attacking a kitten, and peeing inside.

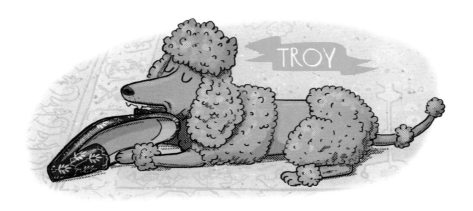

Troy, Parker's last beloved poodle, was by her side when she died in her New York hotel room in 1967.

Behind the scenes, Parker actively campaigned for social justice. She participated in demonstrations and was the national chairperson of the Joint Anti-Fascist Refugee Committee. In her will, she left the bulk of her estate, including the rights to all her work, to civil rights leader Dr. Martin Luther King Jr.

# William Faulkner

---

*Falling Off a Horse*

This southern novelist, winner of the Nobel Prize and two Pulitzer Prizes, really didn't like to talk about literature. His favorite subjects were horses, dogs, and hunting.

From the age of seven, William Faulkner's favorite activity was hunting foxes every November. The fox was sort of beside the point. It was the setting—riding horses at night by torches, the scenic Mississippi countryside—that thrilled him, plus the fellowship with men gathering around a campfire, telling stories.

He went on to create a new world, an imaginary county called Yoknapatawpha County, based on areas where he'd grown up. With *The Sound and the Fury*, *Light in August*, and *As I Lay Dying*, he experimented with style, using language that mimicked thought and endless sentences—one sentence ran 1,800 words.

At his family home in Oxford, Mississippi, he got up early every morning and rode his horse for an hour. If there wasn't a fox hunt going on, he would jump hedges and fences by himself, occasionally falling off or being thrown, breaking his back twice.

He owned various dogs—pointers, Dalmatians, dachshunds—but mostly feists, small scrappy dogs known for their hunting skills.

In his study, he kept a can of Scram Dog Repellent, which he used to keep the dogs away from his prized roses.

He supported his pets in part by working as a successful screenwriter in Hollywood. Though he was emerging as a significant American writer, with the thrill of having his own books adapted for the screen, not everyone caught on. One night he stopped at a bookstore to buy his book of poetry, *A Green Bough*, for a girlfriend. He asked if they had any other William Faulkner books. "No," the clerk said. "Faulkner doesn't sell."

The famous actor Clark Gable once asked him who the best living authors were. Faulkner mentioned Willa Cather, Ernest Hemingway, and himself. Gable asked, "Oh, do you write, Mr. Faulkner?" to which Faulkner replied, "Yeah. What do you do, Mr. Gable?"

Faulkner never gave up writing or riding. One day in 1962, taking a bad spill, he shattered his collarbone. He never really recovered and died a few weeks later.

All the bookstores in Hollywood now have copies of his books.

# E. B. White

—

*Of Dogs, Pigs,
and Spiders*

E.B. White was an American writer famed for his simple but elegant style. A lover of animals, he wrote three classic children's books about them—*Stuart Little*, *Charlotte's Web*, and *The Trumpet of the Swan*.

The only books young E. B. White read were about animals. He started writing at age eight—a poem about his pet mouse, who did tricks and worked out in the gym White built for him. He wrote every day in an unusually thoughtful diary, which he called a "journal," as it sounded more serious.

Dogs were always part of his life. His first one was Mac, a beloved collie. For six years Mac "met me at the same place after school and conveyed me home—a service he thought up himself."

White also raised pigeons, canaries, lizards, and turtles. He was jealous of a friend who had more exotic pets—a monkey and a raccoon.

A box of paper was his idea of a perfect present, almost as good as a new puppy: "A blank piece of paper holds the greatest excitement for me." At 11 he began sending poems and stories to *St. Nicholas Magazine*, a children's magazine that gave many a famous writer a start. Someone told him the magazine was more likely to accept writing that showed kindness to animals. White sent off just such a story, starring a dog, and won a silver medal.

After graduating from Cornell University, he worked as a freelance reporter and writer. He joined the brand-new *New Yorker* weekly magazine when he was 26. With poetry, he wooed and wowed his boss, Katherine Angell, *New Yorker*'s first fiction editor. She had a Scottish terrier, Daisy, and sometimes in his letters and poems he used Daisy's voice, pretending she was the one doing the writing. Katherine was charmed, and they married.

Daisy

*New Yorker* readers loved his witty and meticulously written essays about New York City life, politics, and literature. He used a clear, direct style that showcased his sense of humor. White also contributed poems, cartoon captions, and brief sketches. Over time he became the magazine's most important contributor, just as it was considered the most important literary magazine in America.

Writing was torture for White, "a pure headache." Dogs, including his beloved dachshund, Minnie, eased the pain. He even wrote a poem about a dog, capturing the frenetic way dogs walk on a leash. In fast-paced language, the poem described a dog rushing to sniff everything in sight, yanking the leash every which way.

White was thrilled when he was able to move his family from bustling New York City to a quiet farm in North Brooklin, Maine. He happily devoted himself to raising prize-winning sheep, chickens, pigs, and a whole menagerie of farm animals.

In middle age, he was inspired by animal life on the farm to ease into writing books for children. He started *Stuart Little* at age 45, moving on to *Charlotte's Web* and *The Trumpet of the Swan.* All star lively animals who interact with humans in fascinating ways.

Creator of Charlotte, the most famous spider in literary history, White didn't actually keep spiders as pets. But he did once carefully place a large gray spider and her egg sac in a box he'd prepared. When hundreds of babies hatched atop his dresser and built webs all over his stuff, he found it uniquely thrilling.

Another inspiration for *Charlotte's Web* was the day he discovered that one of his prize pigs had fallen seriously ill. Instead of rushing the pig to the butcher shop to be turned into bacon, he decided to nurse it back to health. He found himself "cast suddenly in the role of pig's friend and physician." The pig unfortunately didn't make it, and aside from influencing *Charlotte*'s plot—"Where's Papa going with that axe?"—the incident resulted in a famous essay, "Death of a Pig."

The story of a spider and a pig remains the top-selling paperback novel for young readers today. It's frequently the first book to move a child to tears: "It is not often that someone comes along who is a true friend and a good writer. Charlotte was both."

In 1941 White and his wife, Katherine, put together an 800-page tome called *A Subtreasury of American Humor.* It included funny stories by Mark Twain, of course, plus White himself and his friend James Thurber.

White also took on the revision of a book by the late William Strunk Jr., *The Elements of Style.* The updated edition became *the* guide for clear writing. The #1 rule: "Omit needless words." The book, informally referred to as *Strunk & White*, plus his own style of writing, were enormously influential.

One day White was accused by the American Society for the Prevention of Cruelty to Animals of not paying a dog tax on Minnie. He couldn't help responding in his finest witty fashion, writing the organization a letter, seemingly very official and business-like, that quickly descended into an exasperated list of Minnie's many foibles and quirks. By bemoaning the great pains he took to care for Minnie, to make her happy and keep her comfortable, White made it humorously clear that he couldn't possibly be guilty of the kind of animal cruelty the agency made it their business to prevent. His letter described dressing Minnie in a knitted sweater for warmth and getting up two or three times a night to adjust the dog's blanket. Great attention is paid to Minnie's desires and whims, like the necessity of a blanket due to Minnie's refusal to wear a bulky sweater to sleep. White stresses his dog's displeasure when she doesn't get enough sleep; in his own account of his duties of care, and his complaint that "I haven't had any real rest in years," it's obvious that White treats his own well-being as less important than Minnie's.

The multitalented White won a Pulitzer Prize special citation for "his letters, essays and the full body of his work." He didn't show up to accept his prize. He had an extreme fear of public speaking and never accepted his many awards in person. Had he ever given a speech, he might have included something he wrote:
"All that I hope to say in books,
all that I ever hope to say, is
that I love the world."

JONES          SUZY

His last two dogs were Jones, a Norwich terrier, and Suzy, a West Highland white terrier. They were with him until his death on his farm in 1985.

# Ernest Hemingway

—

## A Soft Spot
## for Cats

Classic American novelist and short-story writer Ernest Hemingway was awarded the Nobel Prize for Literature in 1954 and is possibly the most widely imitated author ever. He once said, "One cat just leads to another."

Ernest Hemingway carefully cultivated his manly man image. He seemed to be around animals mostly in order to kill them. As an Illinois child he spent his summers in the woods and lakes of northern Michigan, learning to hunt, fish, and camp and developing a passion for outdoor adventure.

But always he had cats as companions, starting with his childhood favorite, Catherine Tiger. He grew up thinking cats were like members of the family. All his life he found them to be great comfort and amusement during times of stress and loneliness, a source of emotional nourishment. His

Catherine Tiger

way of treating them as kings and queens added joy and structure to his solitary pursuit of writing.

Plus cats could be more dependable than humans. "A cat has absolute emotional honesty," he declared. "Human beings, for one reason or another, may hide their feelings, but a cat does not."

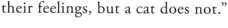

Hemingway gave each a name that seemed to suit its character: Fatso, Friendless (who drank whiskey and milk along with him), Feather Kitty, Sir Winston Churchill, Mooky, Littless Kitty, Furhouse Kitty, Taskforce.

One of his very favorites was Boise, a black-and-white kitten he adopted. He also called him Brother and put him in one of his books. Boise disdained other cats and seemed to think he was human. When he died at 14 of a heart attack, Hemingway grieved and had him buried in a private ceremony.

Hemingway bravely served in both World Wars. During World War I he was an ambulance driver for the American Red Cross. Only 18, he was injured and later decorated for heroism. Upon recovery, he sailed for France as a newspaper reporter.

In Paris he joined a literary circle that included Gertrude Stein, F. Scott Fitzgerald, James Joyce, and others. Stein dubbed them the Lost Generation, unmoored after the war. Helping Hemingway stay balanced was F. Puss, his fat Persian cat. F. Puss made an excellent babysitter to Hemingway's son Jack, nicknamed Bumby, when the adults went out, not allowing anyone near the boy.

In 1925 he published his first important book, a collection of stories called *In Our Time*. The next year *The Sun Also Rises* appeared, and he was on his way to fame, fortune, and a lot of cats. Cats showed up in some of his writings and also influenced nicknames for his wives: Cat, Kat, Kath, Katherine Cat, Kitten, Feather Kitty.

In World War II, he flew several missions with the British Royal Air Force and served with American troops participating in the liberation of Paris. He impressed professional soldiers not only as a man of courage in battle but also as a military expert.

After the war, when not skiing, bullfighting, fishing, hunting on safari, and marrying again (he was married four times), he wrote *A Farewell to Arms* and *For Whom the Bell Tolls,* and he won the Pulitzer Prize for Fiction for *The Old Man and the Sea.* One of his favorite writers was Mark Twain, a fellow cat lover.

He worked best at the crack of dawn. He often wrote standing up, wearing comfy loafers. He had sustained numerous injuries while on his adventures—on safari to Africa, he was almost killed in two separate plane crashes. Writing while standing eased the pain of permanent back problems.

So did the cats who kept him company. He would begin a book by writing in pencil on onionskin paper, and by the second

*Princessa*

or third draft he would switch to a typewriter. Giving him "valuable aid" as he wrote was Princessa, an elegant Persian who was mean to everyone except him.

His style was understated—short sentences from which all adjectives and adverbs had been purged, using repetition and rhythm for emotional effect.

In Cuba, Hemingway enjoyed teaching his cats—notably **Uncle Woofer**—circus tricks, like making cat pyramids.

UNCLE WOOFER

His dialogue was simple and natural sounding. The influence of this style was felt worldwide: writers after Hemingway either imitated him or went out of their way to avoid doing it.

In his lifetime, Hemingway was a celebrity in the style of a famous movie star. He was twice on the cover of *Time* magazine and three times on the cover of *Life*.

One technique that worked well for him was to stop for the day just when the writing was going well: "You write until you come to a place where you still have your juice and know what will happen next and you stop and try to live through the next day until when you hit it again."

At his home in Key West, Florida, he started off with one six-toed kitten named Snowball, an adorable gift from a sea captain. As his cat family grew, it flourished into a whole colony of 23 six-toed kittens. Hemingway called the cats "purr factories" and "love sponges"—not very macho.

Snowball

Today, some 40 to 50 six-toed descendants of Snowball still roam around the Key West house.

When one of the cats, Uncle Willie, was hit by a car, Hemingway had to put him down. "Have had to shoot people but never anyone I knew and loved for eleven years," he mournfully wrote to a friend.

Hemingway moved on to Finca Vigía ("Lookout Farm"), an estate outside Havana, Cuba. At one point he had *57 cats*. At first they lived in the guest bedroom, until he constructed a white tower just for felines. The substantial sum of money that came with the Nobel Prize went toward the care

Cats with six toes are sometimes known simply as **"Hemingway Cats."**

and feeding of cats, including plenty of catnip that he grew himself.

In 1959, seeking a quieter life, he bought a house in Ketchum, Idaho. His last cat was Big Boy Peterson, a loving stray who, like Boise, ate his meals with Hemingway and slept with him every night, rising when he did.

"Good night, my Kitten," were Hemingway's last words to his wife.

Big Boy was probably the last creature to see the writer alive. Two years after moving, he took his own life.

# John Steinbeck

The Famous Charley

John Steinbeck was an American novelist who won the 1962 Nobel Prize for Literature, plus a Pulitzer Prize for *The Grapes of Wrath*. He made his poodle famous in *Travels with Charley*.

Dogs were not always John Steinbeck's best friends.

One awful day, his setter Toby *ate*—"made confetti of"—more than half of the first draft

Toby

of his latest book. Working on paper, before computers, the crisis meant that Steinbeck had to start over. He tried to be philosophical: "Two months work to do over again. It sets me back. There was no other draft. I was pretty mad but the poor little fellow may have been acting critically." Not to worry—*Of Mice and Men*, when completed, went straight to the top of the bestseller list and became a classic.

As a child growing up in central California—the Salad Bowl of the World—Steinbeck was fascinated by pirates and books. The legends of King Arthur and the Knights of the Round Table instilled in him a love for social justice. His favorite writers were Ernest Hemingway, William Faulkner, Jack London, and Robert Louis Stevenson (who wrote one of his favorite books, called *Travels with a Donkey*). He spent his summers working on ranches and later with migrant workers on sugar beet farms.

As a struggling writer accruing many rejections, he supported himself as a manual laborer. His first novel, *Cup of Gold*, based on the life of pirate Henry Morgan, was unsuccessful. Another was rejected by the first seven publishers he sent it to. When the eighth published it, *Tortilla Flat* was an instant success and Steinbeck was moving toward fame and fortune.

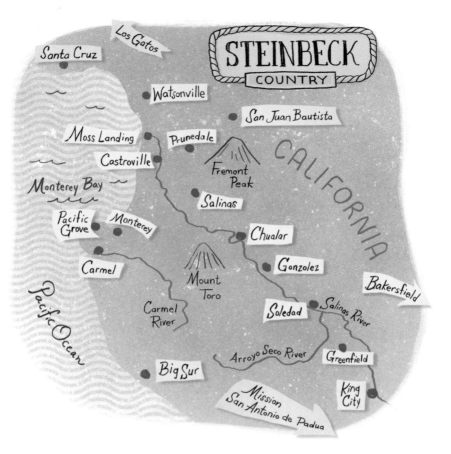

He became best known for *The Grapes of Wrath*, which
aroused widespread sympathy for the plight of migrant
farmworkers. He also wrote *Cannery Row*, *The Pearl*,
*East of Eden*, and *The Winter of Our Discontent*. Salinas,
Monterey, and parts of the San Joaquin Valley in
California were the settings for so many of his stories
that the area is now sometimes referred to as "Steinbeck
Country."

Today many of Steinbeck's works are required reading in American high schools. At the same time, his works have been frequently banned—he was one of the ten most frequently banned authors from 1990 to 2004.

He wrote in longhand on yellow legal pages with sharp pencils, keeping twelve of them at the ready and developing callouses on his fingers. Then he liked to dictate his words for a secretary to transcribe, first playing the tape back for himself: "You can hear the most terrible things you've done if you hear it back clear on tape." His biggest concern was how the words sounded—he was going for "nice sounds"—which explains why so many of his books made great movies.

Dogs kept him company—sometimes they were preferable to humans: "I've seen a look in dogs' eyes, a quickly vanishing look of amazed contempt, and I am convinced that basically dogs think humans are nuts."

Planning a cross-country road trip in his later years, Steinbeck alighted on his French poodle Charley as an ideal fellow traveler. Born on the

CHARLEY

outskirts of Paris, Charley was ten years old, tall with blue-gray hair, and in a rare fight had lost a piece of his right ear. Charley was actually Steinbeck's wife's dog, but she was glad for him to have a companion. The title for the book about their adventure—*Travels with Charley*—was her idea.

He bought a new pickup truck he named Rocinante, after Miguel de Cervantes's horse in *Don Quixote*. He saw himself as a knight in shining armor, a hero on a quest to solve a mystery: "What are Americans like today?" By talking to the locals he met along the way, he wanted to get a clear image of the country. On the truck he installed a specially made camper where he and Charley could sleep when they weren't staying at campgrounds.

Along the journey, Steinbeck treated **Charley** well, with cans of dog food and dog biscuits, stopping a few times for treatments by a vet. In areas where whitetail deer were being hunted, he kept the dog safe by wrapping his tail in red Kleenex and fastening it with rubber bands.

He set off, Charley riding shotgun, from his home in Sag Harbor, New York. He headed from Maine to the Pacific Northwest, down into his native Salinas Valley, across to Texas, up through the Deep South, and then back to New York.

Charley played one role after another on the trip. He excelled as a guard dog, roaring like a lion when a stranger approached the camper. Steinbeck found him great company, believing that Charley was extremely intelligent and could read his mind. He was also the perfect conversation starter with strangers he wanted to talk to—"Oh, what kind of dog is that?" someone would ask.

Charley headed off loneliness and even helped with Steinbeck's work. Using him as a sounding board, Steinbeck talked to him for long periods—nudging him with his foot if the dog nodded off—as a way of exploring his thoughts.

Charley's method for alerting Steinbeck that it was time for a rest stop was to make a "Ftt" sound. Charley would do his business while Steinbeck would poke around to see if anyone or anything interested him.

Charley also devised clever ways to get Steinbeck up at the crack of dawn. If all else failed, he would sit quietly and stare into his face with a sweet and forgiving look: "I come out of deep sleep with the feeling of being looked at…Often the war of wills goes on for quite a time, I squinching my eyes shut and he forgiving me, but he nearly always wins."

Every night Steinbeck wrote up his adventures, shaping them into nonfiction of an unusually creative kind. For example, he wasn't totally roughing it. He did sleep in the camper, but he also stayed in motels a lot, sometimes even luxury hotels, which he didn't mention.

The journey encompassed nearly 10,000 miles and lasted four months. What Steinbeck learned about America left him worried about population shifts, serious racial tension, technological and industrial change, and environmental destruction on an unprecedented scale.

But *Travels with Charley,* published in 1962, became a huge bestseller. It remains in print, regarded by some as an iconic road book, a classic of travel writing, and a superb example of a pet-inspired saga.

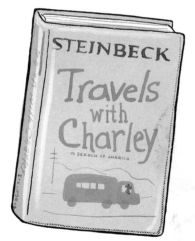

# Marguerite Henry

—

*Queen of the*
*Wild Ponies*

A Midwestern writer, Marguerite Henry was the author of 59 children's books based on true stories of horses and other animals.

At 11, Marguerite Breithaupt sold her first story, about playing hide-and-seek and being found by a clever dog. Her father worked at a publishing company and indulged her with all the writing supplies she could possibly want.

She admired Edgar Allan Poe's use of language and Zane Grey's Western adventures—so many horses. She was once fired from her library job as a "book doctor" (repairing damaged books) for reading too much.

When she married Sidney Henry, he was also supportive of her writing. She went from writing magazine articles to books for children. Pets inspired her—a dachshund named Alex, a poodle named Patrick Henry—and she kept her walls covered with pictures of horses, cats, and dogs.

Her most famous book, *Misty of Chincoteague,* was inspired by a real-life wild pony. *Misty* brings to life the annual roundup of wild ponies swimming from Assateague Island to Chincoteague, off the coast of Virginia and Maryland. Henry was able to bring Misty home to Illinois with her. She built a stable, and local

kids competed to clean and groom her. With excellent
manners, Misty sometimes even appeared in Henry's
living room to greet special visitors.

When *Misty* came out in 1947, bookstores couldn't
keep it in stock. Henry wore fanciful hats, like one of
artificial flowers with animals peeking out, to book
signings. *Misty* was named an honor book for the
Newbery Medal, as was *Justin Morgan Had a Horse*,
while the actual medal later went to her book *King of
the Wind*, the story of an Arabian stallion.

Henry's last book was *Brown Sunshine of Sawdust Valley*,
a novel published in 1996 when she was 94 years old.
She died the next year—that's 83 years of writing
about animals.

# Pablo Neruda

—

## When Your Pet
## Saves Your Life

The most important Latin American
poem—one whose life was saved by a
dog—Pablo Neruda is famous for love
poems, epic historical poems, poems
about ordinary animals and objects, and
especially poems of fighting unfairness.

A mere 10 years after being born in 1904 in Chile, a boy named Neftali began to scribble poems. By 13, he had published an essay.

At 20, with two books of poems published, he was one of the best-known Chilean poets. His father, a railway worker, so strongly disapproved of poetry—a sure path to poverty—that Neftali disguised himself. He used a pseudonym, or pen name: Pablo Neruda.

When he wasn't horseback riding, Neruda kept on writing all kinds of poems. With a strong love for his country, he often challenged the wealthy aristocracy, which he faulted for harming ordinary people. He penned his poetry in green ink, believing it was the color of hope.

Then as now, it was extremely difficult to make a living with poetry—Neruda needed a day job. He worked his way into politics, becoming a diplomat representing

Chile all over the world, often in countries where people were rebelling against cruel governments.

On a diplomatic post to Spain, he was met at the Madrid train station by someone he greatly admired, famed poet Federico García Lorca. The Spanish Civil War was about to break out, a serious crisis pitting the monarchy against the people. An idealistic, progressive spirit was galvanizing writers, especially Lorca, who passed it on to his friend. Neruda was coming out of a period of depression and isolation from serving in a series of posts in East Asia. He craved the companionship of his fellow activists and artists.

Then, early on in the war, Lorca was executed by government forces. The news dealt a huge shock to Neruda. It wasn't just the horror of a friend's assassination. Lorca's death was something more: he seemed to symbolize all of poetry, so it was as if

FREDERICO GARCÍA LORCA

enemies had assassinated poetry itself.

No more sad verses for Neruda, love poems sprinkled with red poppies, or dreamy experiments, all of which ignored the realities of ugly forces rising around the world. Now he wanted bold, repeated words and clear, vivid images to communicate in a way that could be understood immediately by a wide audience. In his poem "I Explain Some Things" he announced his simpler style, one that would compel others into action.

One of Neruda's greatest works was a monumental book of poems called *Canto General.* It was a unique, epic history "of the Americas … [told from] the point of view of the people themselves, not the history told by the conquerors."

Kiria

For a time Neruda kept a beloved tame mongoose, **Kiria**, as a pet. She ate at his table, trampled his papers, and took her siesta curled up on his shoulders. He was devastated the day she disappeared.

As bombs fell over Madrid, killing innocent civilians, Neruda moved to Paris. There he helped organize a gigantic gathering of writers to express solidarity with the Spanish people. Fellow writers Ernest Hemingway and Langston Hughes were among those who joined him.

Neruda's proudest accomplishment (besides his poems) took place in Paris. He was able to coordinate the escape of 2,000 Spanish refugees. They had been housed by the French in filthy camps, but he was able to get them to Chile on an old ship. Headlines across the world applauded him. He called it "the noblest mission I have ever undertaken."

Besides being a poet and an activist, Neruda was also an animal lover. He never skipped a visit to the zoo in whatever city he was in.

And pets were important. He tried keeping a pet badger, but it had a habit of biting guests in the neck, so it had to go.

His most beloved pet was Kuthaka, a dog who literally saved his life. One night, near where he was living in Sri Lanka, Neruda stumbled during a nighttime stroll with his dog. He fell onto the rails right in front of an oncoming train. Luckily, Kuthaka's loud barking alerted the train driver to stop in time. In honor of his dog's heroism, Neruda called the pet dogs he owned in his later years in Chile by the same name.

Kuthaka

Perhaps he was thinking of Kuthaka when he wrote an elegy of great sadness: his poem "A Dog Has Died." It was a heartbreaking requiem that described many of the happy, joyful qualities of a person's relationship with a beloved dog, but in the past tense–comfort and solace that the dog can provide him no longer. Neruda described the special gaze that a dog gave only to its owner in his poem, and the selfless love and companionship that dogs offer without demanding anything in return.

As his poems sold more and more around the world, Neruda used his platform to speak out for social justice. His views sometimes put him on the wrong side of his own government. He would be fired from his posts or would have to go into hiding to avoid arrest, with manuscripts in the saddlebags on the horse spiriting him across the mountains. Once he spent three years in exile.

One particularly frightening night, his house was raided by Chilean armed forces. Neruda got out of his bed and faced them down, saying, "Look around— there's only one thing of danger for you here—poetry." The police backed off.

How much power can poetry have? A lot, Neruda believed. One poem alone cannot stop a war or remove a bad ruler. But poetry has such a unique way of distilling truths. Its power is cumulative: one by one, like drops of water, poems splash into people's brains. Neruda believed that poetry *could* be dangerous, with a role to play in the overall efforts of resistance to unfairness.

In San Francisco, during a 2003 antiwar demonstration, Neruda's inspiring words were spelled out on banners draping the streets: "Tyranny cuts off the head that sings, but the voice at the bottom of the well returns to the secret springs of the earth and out of the darkness rises up through the mouth of the people."

His words were also spray-painted on the streets of Cairo, Egypt, during the Arab Spring demonstrations

starting in 2010: "You can cut all the flowers, but you cannot stop spring from coming." During the January 2017 Women's Marches around the world, women held posters with those same words.

Neruda was awarded the Nobel Prize for Literature in 1971. His works had been translated into many languages all over the world, earning him enough income to own three houses.

By the time of his death in 1973, he was considered the national poet of Chile. He was famous *and* rich—no mean feat for a poet.

# Kurt Vonnegut

—

Black Humor with
a Pumpkin Accent

Blending techniques of fantasy and science fiction to depict the horrors of modern life, Kurt Vonnegut had a grim, even morbid point of view—except when it came to his little dog Pumpkin.

As a child, Kurt Vonnegut wrote pages and pages in his diary, even though "nothing ever happened to me." Serving in the US Air Force during World War II, he was captured by the Germans. The 1945 bombing of Dresden, Germany, which killed some 25,000 civilians and leveled the city, happened during his captivity. He survived by sheltering in a locker in a slaughterhouse—surrounded by animal cadavers.

His first novel, *Player Piano*, was not a success. But he persisted, with *Cat's Cradle* (about the threat of nuclear destruction, not an actual cat) and more, perfecting his black humor, which was funny but also despairing. His influences were George Orwell, Mark Twain, and his mother, who had tried writing for magazines. His breakthrough was *Slaughterhouse-Five*, based on his Dresden nightmare. An immediate bestseller, it had a famous refrain—"So it goes"—generally used after a death.

Cheering Vonnegut up was Pumpkin, his Lhasa apso, a barky breed with comically long hair. Pumpkin napped on his lap in the study, frolicked on the beach, went for walks in the rain (Vonnegut held the umbrella for Pumpkin, not himself), and was included in wedding photos. Animals seemed superior to people: "Ask anybody. Dogs and cats are smarter than we are," Vonnegut wrote. As he became antiwar, he extended his pacifism to animals, refusing to hunt or fish.

After Pumpkin died, Vonnegut got another Lhasa apso, Flour. In 2007, at age 84, he was walking Flour when he tripped on the leash, fell outside his New York home, and later died.

"And how should we behave during this Apocalypse?" he once asked. "We should be unusually kind to one another, certainly. But we should also stop being so serious. Jokes help a lot. And get a dog, if you don't already have one."

Flour

# Flannery O'Connor

---

*Life Is Better with Peacocks*

An American writer in a darkly comic Southern gothic style, Flannery O'Connor wrote two novels and thirty-two short stories considered masterpieces—and she was also famous for collecting peafowl.

Flannery O'Connor didn't outline her stories in advance: "I just kind of feel [the story] out like a hound-dog," she said. "I follow the scent."

In her writing she may have imitated a hound dog, but otherwise her life was all about fowl. Namely, how did she come to live with 100 peafowl?

It all started with one chicken. She later described herself, growing up on a Georgia farm, as "a pigeon-toed only-child with a receding chin and a you-leave-me-alone-or-I'll-bite-you complex." Somehow, at age five, she trained a Cochin bantam chicken to walk backward—such a bizarre feat that it attracted widespread publicity.

One day, a photographer from New York showed up. He put both O'Connor and the chicken into a short film—*Unique Chicken Goes in Reverse*—to be shown in between movies in theaters.

That day marked O'Connor's obsession with collecting chickens and other fowl. She even began to make them clothes. Colonel Eggbert, a gray bantam, had his own white piqué coat with a lace collar and two buttons in the back. Instead of her high school assignment—sewing a Sunday dress for herself—O'Connor sewed a full outfit of clothes to fit her pet duck, complete with duck underwear, and brought the duck to school to model it.

*Colonel Eggbert*

She couldn't stop, and she went on to acquire pheasants, quails, turkeys, emus, ostriches, seventeen geese, a tribe of mallard ducks, three Japanese silky bantams, and several chickens—Polish crested and Rhode Island Red.

Meanwhile, graduating from Georgia State College for Women and studying creative writing at the University of Iowa Writers' Workshop, she found success with words. She loved the work of Nathaniel Hawthorne, Edgar Allan Poe, and Henry James. O'Connor put her own spin on her idols while working as a babysitter to pay the rent. Her novels—like the first, *Wise Blood*— and short stories were usually set in the rural American South. They were disturbing, with startling acts of violence and plenty of bird imagery.

In her twenties, despite never having seen or heard them, O'Connor developed a sudden craving for peafowl, especially peacocks. To attract mates, she knew, the males of the species possessed magnificent tails that seemed to unfurl a map of the solar system. She mail-ordered six peacocks, a peahen, and four peachicks.

When they arrived, she was so jazzed that she declared, "I want so many of them that every time I go out the door I'll run into one." As the peafowl mated, her wish came to pass. She was surrounded.

She adored observing the mating ritual,

with the peacock
strutting about and
putting on his glittering
show and the females ignoring him. She took notes on
everything else about their behavior. Sometimes they
sang along to recordings of Chopin that she played.
They seemed to have violent dreams. Calls and answers
echoed through the night, screams that sounded like
"Help! Help!" and made their way into her stories.

She enjoyed the reactions of others to her unusual pets:
"Visitors to our place, instead of being barked at by
dogs rushing from under the porch, are squalled at by
peacocks whose blue necks and crested heads pop up
from behind tufts of grass, peer out of bushes and crane
downward from the roof of the house." The mating
ritual usually met with an awed silence: "When
it suits him, the peacock will face you. Then you
will see in a green-bronze arch around him a
galaxy of gazing haloed suns. This is the moment
when most people are silent."

Groups of first-graders often visited her, many of them pointing as a peacock swung around: "Oh, look at his underwear!"

At age 25, O'Connor suddenly felt a heaviness in her "typing arms." It was the first sign of lupus, a serious, painful disorder of the immune system that weakens the muscles. Told that she would live only another four years, she buckled down to work. Her attitude was positive: "The disease is of no consequence to my writing, since for that I use my head and not my feet."

For the rest of her life, she lived with her mother at the family farm in Alabama. She worked in the morning, being too tired and foggy to work later. If necessary, she would rest for 22 hours so that she could write for two, nibbling vanilla wafers, her preferred snack. She often discarded her work of the previous day: "Sometimes I work for months and have to throw everything away, but I don't think any of that was time wasted."

It became harder and harder for her to walk, but if she was up to it she would take care of the birds and receive visitors. Standing over her pets on her crutches, she seemed to find a source of peace in them and perhaps a spur to help her keep her positive attitude and give her strength.

Despite her illness, she managed to give frequent speeches about her work. During one of her talks, a girl asked, "Miss O'Connor, why do you write?"

"Because I'm good at it" was the reply.

When she finally had to be admitted to a hospital, the doctors forbade her to write. But she hid a notebook under her pillow, taking it out when the nurses weren't around.

Having lived 13 years with lupus, she died in 1964 at age 39.

Six years later, her *Complete Stories* won the National Book Award for Fiction.

# Maurice Sendak

—

*Dogs and Other Wild Things*

Often considered the most important children's book author of the 20th century, Maurice Sendak created the Caldecott Medal–winning *Where the Wild Things Are*. Many of his brilliant books were about animals—which he also loved in person.

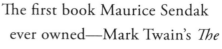

The first book Maurice Sendak ever owned—Mark Twain's *The Prince and the Pauper*—was given to him by his sister. He devoured comic books, Charlie Chaplin movies, monster movies, and Walt Disney's *Mickey Mouse* and *Fantasia*. A sickly child, he started writing his own stories at age nine. His big break came right after high school graduation, when he got his dream job—designing window displays at the F. A. O. Schwarz toy store in New York City—while taking art classes.

His windows caught the attention of legendary children's book editor Ursula Nordstrom. She hired him to illustrate *The Wonderful Farm* in 1951—and the rest is history. He went on to illustrate more than 80 acclaimed books by various writers before penning his own thoroughly original stories to illustrate. Dogs inspired many of Sendak's books throughout his long and distinguished career. He declared that

*Higglety Pigglety Pop! Or There Must Be More to Life* was his personal favorite. The inspiration for it was his own dog, a Sealyham terrier named Jennie, also the name of the main character. The real Jennie died just before the book was published.

JENNIE

Once, when a visitor came to his New York apartment to meet Jennie and Sendak's cat, the visitor mentioned that cats made him sneeze. Sendak politely put his cat out on the window ledge—and unfortunately it was never seen again.

In his masterpiece, *Where the Wild Things Are,* he created creatures based on immigrant relatives who looked like gargoyles and frightened him as a child. It was a most unusual book, a "wild rumpus" that addressed real emotions that children feel, including anger and sadness. Some critics thought it was too scary for kids. But it went on to sell millions and millions of copies, becoming a staple of childhood—a book that everyone reads at some point. It was the first in Sendak's famous trilogy, followed by *In the Night Kitchen* and *Outside Over There.*

Melville

One of his most important pet dogs was Melville, a sweet-tempered German shepherd, named after one of his literary idols, Herman Melville. (Other idols were Emily

Dickinson, the Brothers Grimm, and Beatrix Potter.) For a long time he wanted to write a story using one of Melville's own titles. *Moby-Dick* didn't quite work, and he finally hit on *Pierre*, a lesser-known Melville title that he put his own spin on, creating a bossy, obnoxious child.

Sendak once admitted to an audience, "I hate people." Instead, he said, he preferred the company of dogs like Melville.

He could seem curmudgeonly. But he was also extremely encouraging to new artists, acting as mentor to many. Close friends called him "unbelievably hilarious" and an excellent mimic, with a wicked sense of humor. He had firm likes and dislikes. He hated ebooks, for example. He couldn't stand the term "kiddie books."

He and his partner of 50 years moved from the city to the wilds of Connecticut, where they took up gardening and got themselves more dogs. Dogs seemed to bring out Sendak's soft side.

When visitors came to his Connecticut home, they were greeted by Agamemnon (Aggie), a large German shepherd bounding straight at them. Visitors soon realized how friendly Aggie was. Sendak also had Erda, another German shepherd, and Io, a retriever. Aggie and Erda starred in *Some Swell Pup: or Are Sure You Want a Dog?,* a guide to raising puppies.

He would take guests for long rambles in the forest. If they came across a rabbit in the woods, it would inspire a lecture about Beatrix Potter. He'd head for his library and pull out his first edition of *Peter Rabbit* and show how a rabbit on paper could be as alive as the one they'd just seen. He even owned a walking stick that once belonged to Potter.

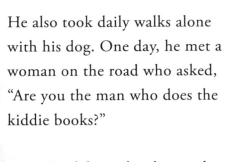

He also took daily walks alone with his dog. One day, he met a woman on the road who asked, "Are you the man who does the kiddie books?"

Sendak tried to keep calm. He deliberately didn't write sunshine and rainbow books, and he didn't like to be talked down to.

So he growled that yes he was, but that he was too busy to talk.

"Do you want to know what I think of them?" she said. "I think they're terrible!" "I think *you're* terrible!" he shot back—and went back home to his dogs and his books.

That woman was in the minority, as Sendak had by then won worldwide acclaim and too many awards to count. His work had changed the whole shape of children's literature.

One of his favorites of all the gifts given to him by fans was a furry stuffed mouse that he named Beatrix, after Beatrix Potter. He kept the mouse beside him on his drawing table as he worked, blasting operas and sonatas and anything by Mozart on his fancy stereo system. He took Beatrix with him whenever he traveled, and when she became too raggedy to travel he took the rock on which she perched.

Sendak was laboring on a picture book about an angry boy named **Max** (also the name of Sendak's German shepherd). It was called *Where the Wild Horses Are*—until one day he decided he really didn't draw horses very well. "Horses" became "Things."

Somewhere along the way he changed its name from Beatrix to Judy. Before he died in 2012, he made a friend promise that "Judy the mouse" would be cremated along with him upon his death.

Unfortunately for historians, Sendak's will directed his "executors to destroy, immediately following my death, all of my personal letters, journals and diaries." But he left all of his original paintings to libraries, where others could study them.

And he made sure his dogs went to his closest friend.

# Alice Walker

—

Communing with
Chickens

A lover and keeper of chickens and one of the most prominent African American authors, novelist, short story writer, poet, and activist Alice Walker is most famous for the novel *The Color Purple*, which won the Pulitzer Prize.

Alice Walker was the eighth child of African American sharecroppers in rural Georgia. She had two strong connections with chickens as she was growing up. One was the gift of music lessons, for which her family could pay with eggs from their Rhode Island Red chickens.

And one of her weekly chores, at 9 or 10, was to chase the chicken the family was going to have for dinner and wring its neck: "Knowing me to be excruciatingly tender-hearted," she wrote later, "as a child this must have wrecked a part of me."

She was excused from many farm chores because of an eye disability. She had been accidentally blinded in one eye by one of her brothers shooting a BB gun during a game.

It was after the eye injury that Walker turned inward and took up reading and writing. By 15 she had compiled an ambitious scrapbook of poetry titled *Poems of a Childhood Poetess*.

Walker attended the only high school in her area that would accept black children. She went on to become its top student, winning a college scholarship and being voted most popular student of her graduating class as well as prom queen.

She left for college in 1961 with three things that her mother gave her: a sewing machine that symbolized self-sufficiency and independence; a suitcase, which she took as permission to travel the world; and most important of all, a typewriter, so she could write down her mother's and her own stories.

On the way to college, her rebelliousness and activism began to stir. Black people were compelled by the law at the time to sit in the back of any bus. Inspired by the civil rights movement and speeches by the Rev. Dr. Martin Luther King Jr., whom she had seen over the summer, she deliberately chose a seat in the front of the bus. A white woman complained to the bus driver, and Walker was forced to take a seat in the back.

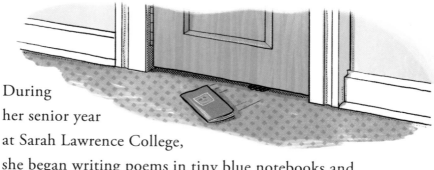

During
her senior year
at Sarah Lawrence College,
she began writing poems in tiny blue notebooks and
slipping them under the office door of her professor, the
poet Muriel Rukeyser. Rukeyser showed the poems to
her agent, and a collection of them was published four
years later when Walker was 24.

Margaret Walker

In most of her literature courses in
college, Walker was not taught a single
work written by an African American.
Finally, she took a class with Margaret
Walker, a poet who was part of the
Chicago Black Renaissance. She learned
about Zora Neale Hurston, a writer
and anthropologist crucial to the Harlem Renaissance
movement in the 1920s. Hurston would profoundly
influence Walker, as did other writers like Virginia Woolf
and Flannery O'Connor.

In 1973, before becoming editor of *Ms. Magazine*,
Walker hunted for Zora Neale Hurston's unmarked

grave in Florida. After making sure the grave got a distinguished marker, Walker did all she could to revive interest in Hurston's work and bring all her works back into print.

After graduating, Walker moved to Mississippi and became involved in the civil rights movement. She also began teaching, creating a class for the study of African American women writers, the first-known class of its kind in the country.

She published well-received short stories, essays, and novels, most notably her masterpiece, *The Color Purple*, about a black woman's battle for survival and independence. With intense insights into African American culture, her work takes on the struggles of black people, particularly women, and their lives in a racist, sexist, and violent society. A feminist herself, Walker coined the term "womanist" in 1983 to mean a black feminist or feminist of color.

She moved to an apple-farming area in Northern California with her dog, Marley, and her cat, Surprise.

Mostly she kept chickens—a lot of chickens. She was in Bali after *The Color Purple* came out as a movie (starring Oprah Winfrey), coming back from a fire dance, when she saw a chicken. Suddenly she remembered the connections she used to have with chickens.

Her chickens were literary birds—she named her first one Gertrude, after the writer Gertrude Stein. Gertrude was always her favorite. Other names were more playful—Glorious, Rufus, Splendor, Hortensia (so tough she would eat her own eggs), Babe, Agnes of God, and five named Gladys.

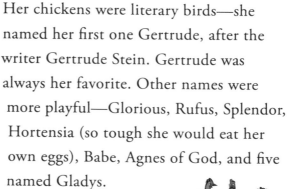

Before much time had passed, watering and feeding the chickens, she had fallen in love with them, finding them "undeniably gorgeous."

At one point Walker had as many as twelve chickens. She built them a deluxe, well-ventilated condo filled with straw, electric lights, and a wall heater. She thought about installing a TV for them to watch. She kept them well fed—with sunflower seeds, grapes, cracked corn, pears, and kale—and scraped out the poop herself with a spatula.

She liked to put her feet up on a green stool and just observe them: "They cuddle! Two or three will sit in my lap at one time. Who knew? It's like finding a whole other area of animal love that we never knew existed."

Perhaps surprisingly, Walker didn't have qualms about eating eggs from her beloved **chickens**—"I just love you more with every bite."

The relationship deepened. "Good morning, girls, it's Mommy!" she would greet them each day. She let them balance on her shoulders, always wearing glasses because she knew they pecked at anything shiny—eyeballs, for example. She lectured them when they behaved badly. Sometimes she sang along with them or read to them from the *I Ching*, the ancient Chinese book of philosophical teachings. She mourned whenever one died.

Chickens began infiltrating her thoughts, and she ended up writing a whole book about this new relationship. Page after page detailed her observations about their daily lives. She included poems and letters she wrote them when she had to travel.

ALICE WALKER

THE CHICKEN CHRONICLES

Chickens became a way for her to talk about other things, like her reflections about events in the news, the interdependence of humans and animals, and memories of her childhood. She wrote about Indian activist Mahatma Gandhi, wrote a tribute to singer Michael Jackson, and delved into the mysteries of life and mysteries about herself: "Over the months they pecked open places I hadn't been able to enter by myself." She thought of them as teachers and angels.

While Alice Walker communes with her chickens, *The Color Purple* remains one of the five most read books in America.

# J. K. Rowling

—

*The Best Reason to
Have a Pet*

A lifelong pet lover, British writer J. K. Rowling is super famous for seven books about Harry Potter, the Boy Who Lived, books bursting with animals, real and imaginary.

When Joanne Rowling was four and sick with measles, her dad read her Kenneth Grahame's *The Wind in the Willows*. The book was all about friendships among Mole, Rat, Mr. Toad, and Badger.

By six she was making her own book, a story about a rabbit, called *Rabbit*. She turned it into a series (a habit of hers) and read it to her younger sister. Her main influence was Richard Scarry and his animal books, especially *I Am a Bunny*.

She'd always wanted a real rabbit, but her first pet was

a dog called Thumper (named after the rabbit in Disney's *Bambi*). When he became ill and had to be put to sleep, she was so sad she can still remember the feeling. She also had tropical fish, two guinea pigs (alas, eaten by a fox), and another dog, Misty, who kept her company until she went away to college.

Rowling later said that she based the character of Hermione Granger, a main character in her Harry Potter books, on herself when she was 11. That was the age Rowling wrote her first novel, about seven cursed diamonds and the people who owned them. She was the first to admit it had no plot or character development.

To get better at writing, she read like crazy. Early on she loved *The Lion, the Witch and the Wardrobe* by C. S. Lewis and *The Little White Horse* by Elizabeth Goudge (a fantasy with several clear influences on Harry Potter). Jane Austen became her favorite author, with *Emma* her favorite book of hers.

At the University of Exeter, wearing heavy black eye makeup and dark goth clothes, she didn't study much, preferring to read Charles Dickens and J. R. R. Tolkien on her own. While reading Dickens's *A Tale of Two Cities*, she couldn't stop crying at its last line: "It is a far, far better thing that I do, than I have ever done; it is a far, far better rest that I go to than I have ever known."

After working for Amnesty International as a researcher and secretary, she detoured to Portugal to teach English. But after a brief marriage and the birth of her daughter Jessica, she settled in Edinburgh, Scotland.

Rowling had her Harry Potter brainstorm in 1990 while sitting on a delayed train. She couldn't find a working pen, or even eye makeup, to write with, so she forced herself to detail it in her mind. When she got home she wrote it all down in a small cheap notebook. Later, while on a plane, she thought up the four houses of Hogwarts and wrote them on the back of an airsickness bag.

Over the next five years, she mapped out all seven books of the series. The final book's last chapter was one of the earliest things she wrote. She wrote mostly in longhand, scribbling on odd scraps that she stashed in shoeboxes.

She wrote in the Elephant House and other cafés, wherever she could get baby Jessica to fall asleep. Living on assistance from the government, dealing with being a single mother, she labored alone. "I was the biggest failure I knew," she said.

The manuscript that became *Harry Potter and the Sorcerer's Stone* was submitted to twelve publishing houses. All of them rejected it, much to their later regret. When another publisher finally said yes, Rowling was advised to get a day job, since she had little chance of making money in children's books. The publisher printed a mere 1,000 copies.

Her publisher recommended a gender-neutral pen name to make sure boys wouldn't be put off. She had no middle name but added her grandmother's, Kathleen, and became J. K. Rowling. (Later, with some of her adult books, she became Robert Galbraith to distinguish those from her children's books.)

Just before the first Harry Potter book came out, she won a nice grant from the Scottish Arts Council, which gave her a lifelong gratitude to Scotland. For the first time, Rowling could afford her own pets—tropical fish, a cat named Chaos, a rabbit (at last) named Jemima, and a guinea pig named Jasmine.

Dogs were her favorite as she built the Harry Potter universe. Butch, a Jack Russell terrier, accompanied her to pick out a companion: Sapphire, a rescued greyhound. Sapphire couldn't decide whether

*Sapphire*

*Butch*

Once fans saw the bond between Harry and his owl **Hedwig**, the sale of real owls soared. But owls don't actually make good pets; they're dangerous and too often abandoned. Rowling had a suggestion: "If your owl-mania seeks concrete expression, why not sponsor an owl at a bird sanctuary."

to be in the same room as her or not, so Rowling had to spend precious Harry Potter writing time constantly getting up to open the door and then close it again.

*Harry Potter* sparked like lightning and became a publishing legend. The last book in the series was the fastest-selling book of all time. The books have been translated into 65 languages and are credited with generating a whole new interest in reading among kids (as well as adults).

In 2004, Rowling was named the first person to become a billionaire by writing books. She has since been demoted from that status because she gives so much money to charity. But she remains quite wealthy, able to buy whatever pets she likes.

Characters in the series (notably Hagrid, the gamekeeper) have lots of animals, from pet rats and cats to the more fantastical—a phoenix, hippogriffs, unicorns, dragons, and owls with unusual powers.

Brontë

In real life—living in Edinburgh with her second husband, their two children, and Jessica—she remains a dog lover. Her West Highland white terrier is named Brontë, after writer Anne Brontë (not quite as famous as her sisters Emily and Charlotte). The name could also be short for Brontosaurus: "She's hardly ever called 'Brontë,' though. The very opposite of She-Who-Must-Not-Be-Named, she's got about a hundred nicknames."

An avid Tweeter, Rowling tweets about Scottish politics, American politics, rugby, her many charities, Potter trivia—and Brontë. She tweeted pictures of

Brontë resting on her keyboard: "When your dog decides you've written enough for one day." Or in another pose: "Patiently waiting for mom to make her a main character."

To the trendy Twitter account WeRateDogs, she submitted pics of Brontë looking adorable and windswept on a boat. Users were quick to award the pup a score of 13/10—true celebrity status. Rowling tweeted happily that she'd been suffering from a bout of writer's block, which the good news cured.

The best possible reason for a writer to have a pet.

# Glossary

**Black Humor**: Also called dark humor or gallows humor; a style of humor that makes light of topics generally considered too difficult and uncomfortable to joke about, including death, disease, and suffering.

**Cliffhanger Ending**: In a story told in several parts, a cliffhanger is a suspenseful ending that leaves a story's characters in peril (such as hanging from a cliff...hence the name) to make readers come back for the next installment.

**Editor**: An author's collaborator and sounding board. The editor is the first reader of the work and a rigorous partner who gives feedback to help the author find their best self-expression.

**Elegy**: A poem of lamentation in honor of someone who has died. An elegy bemoans the deceased, celebrates their life, and consoles the reader.

**Epic**: A style of poem that tells the story of an adventure, often spanning many years and crossing many lands, featuring a large cast of characters.

**Gothic Fiction**: A genre of literature that combines themes of death, romance, horror, and sometimes even the supernatural.

**Nobel Prize**: One of the world's most prestigious awards, Nobel Prizes are awarded for work in literature, science, the pursuit of peace, and other fields.

**Novel**: A fictional story told in prose, long enough to fill a book, following a set of characters through a series of connected events in their lives.

**Poetry**: A form of literature expressed in verses, whether conforming to a specific metered structure or in the form of free verse. Poetry is a medium that can narrate a story or simply express ideas and feelings.

**Prose**: A medium of written expression that doesn't conform to verse or meter like poetry, but flows naturally, the way language is spoken.

**Pseudonym**: An artificial name used by an author to hide their identity.

**Pulitzer Prize**: Another of the world's most prestigious awards, the Pulitzer Prize is awarded for work in literature, journalism, and music.

**Stream of Consciousness:**
A style of writing that
approximates the mind's
innermost thoughts, where
one idea leads to another
and another, sometimes
incongruously, or
unbroken by conventional
sentence structure or even
punctuation.

**Writer's Block:** A common affliction for authors and poets, a total creative paralysis. Writers stricken with this temporary mental block sit in front of a blank page but can't make anything come out.

# More Books About These Great Writers

Adams, Maureen B. *Shaggy Muses: The Dogs Who Inspired Virginia Woolf, Emily Dickinson, Elizabeth Barrett Browning, Edith Wharton and Emily Brontë.* Chicago: University of Chicago Press, 2007.

Brennen, Carlene Fredericka. *Hemingway's Cats: An Illustrated Biography.* Sarasota, FL: Pineapple Press, 2005.

Clemens, Clara. *My Father, Mark Twain.* New York: Harper, 1931.

Collins, David R. *Write a Book for Me: The Story of Marguerite Henry.* Greensboro, NC: Morgan Reynolds, 1999.

Currey, Mason. *Daily Rituals: How Artists Work.* New York: Knopf, 2013.

Gherman, Beverly. *E. B. White: Some Writer.* New York: Atheneum, 1992.

Gigliotti, Jim. *Who Was Edgar Allan Poe?* New York: Grosset, 2015.

Gooch, Brad. *Flannery: A Life of Flannery O'Connor.* New York: Little, Brown, 2009.

Johnson, Celia Blue. *Odd Type Writers: From Joyce and Dickens to Wharton and Welty, the Obsessive Habits and Quirky Techniques of Great Authors.* New York: Perigee, 2013.

Kirk, Connie Ann. *J. K. Rowling: A Biography.* Westport, CT: Greenwood Press, 2003.

Krull, Kathleen. *Lives of the Writers: Comedies, Tragedies (and What the Neighbors Thought).* New York: Harcourt, 1997.

Lear, Linda J. *Beatrix Potter: A Life in Nature.* New York: St. Martin's, 2007.

Meade, Marion. *Dorothy Parker: What Fresh Hell Is This?* New York: Penguin, 1987.

O'Connor, Flannery. *"The King of the Birds," in Mystery and Manners.* New York: Farrar, Straus, 1969.

Ryan, Pam Munoz. *The Dreamer.* New York: Scholastic, 2010.

Stein, Gertrude. *The Autobiography of Alice B. Toklas.* New York: Random House, 1960.

Steinbeck, John. *Travels with Charley: In Search of America.* New York: Viking, 1962.

Tracy, Kathleen. *John Steinbeck.* Hockessin, DE: Mitchell Lane, 2005.

Walker, Alice. *The Chicken Chronicles.* New York: New Press, 2011.

Woolf, Virginia. *Flush: A Biography.* New York: Harcourt, 1933.

# Citations

Illustrator Violet Lemay has respectfully interpreted the beautiful book covers, illustrations, and sketches of the great authors and artists to whom this book pays tribute.

**Introduction:** p. 6 excerpt from a poem by Julia Jones, *Rail Cadet*, 2018.

**Edgar Allan Poe:** p. 22 cover of *The Raven* by Edgar Allan Poe with commentary by Edmund Clarence Stedman, illustrated by Gustave Doré, Harper & Brothers, 1884.

**Mark Twain:** p. 39 *The Jumping Frog* by Mark Twain, illustrated by F. Strothman, Harper & Brothers, 1904; p. 43 ad for Bambino written by Mark Twain for the *New York American*, 1905; p. 45 brochure cover from Twain's Around the World tour of the British colonies (photographer unknown), 1895–1896.

**Beatrix Potter:** pp. 51, 52, 53 various sketches by Beatrix Potter, c. 1875; p. 54 Christmas card drawn by Beatrix and Bertram Potter, c. 1890; p. 55 letter from Beatrix Potter to Noel Moore with rabbit drawings, 1893; p. 56 *The Tale of*

*Peter Rabbit* by Beatrix Potter, privately printed, 1901.

**Virginia Woolf**: p. 76 *Flush: A Biography*, written by Virginia Woolf, illustrated by Vanessa Bell, The Hogarth Press, 1933.

**E. B. White**: p. 97 *The Trumpet of the Swan* by E. B. White, illustrated by Edward Frascino, Harper & Row, 1970; *Charlotte's Web* by E. B. White, illustrated by Garth Williams, Harper & Brothers, 1952; *Stuart Little* by E. B. White, illustrated by Garth Williams, Harper & Brothers, 1945.

**John Steinbeck**: p. 121 *Travels with Charley: In Search of America* by John Steinbeck, The Viking Press, 1962.

**Marguerite Henry**: p. 123 *Misty of Chincoteague* by Marguerite Henry, illustrated by Wesley Dennis, Rand McNally and Company, 1947.

**Pablo Neruda**: p. 135 graffiti in Arabic by Bahia Shehab from a Neruda poem: "You can cut all the flowers, but you cannot stop spring from coming."

**Maurice Sendak**: p. 149 *Where the Wild Things Are* by Maurice Sendak, Harper & Row, 1963; p. 150 *The Prince and the Pauper* by Mark Twain, James R. Osgood & Co., 1882; p. 153 *Pierre: A Cautionary Tale in Five Chapters and a Prologue* by Maurice Sendak, Scholastic, 1962.

**Alice Walker**: p. 163 *The Color Purple* by Alice Walker, Harcourt Brace Jovanovich, New York, 1982; p. 166 *The Authentic I Ching: The Essential Guide to Reading and Using* *the I Ching* by Dr. Wang Yang and Jon Sandifer, Watkins, 1999; *The Chicken Chronicles: Sitting with the Angels Who Have Returned with My Memories* by Alice Walker, cover art by Jules Frazier/Getty Images, Weidenfeld & Nicholson, 2011.

**J. K. Rowling**: p. 170 *The Wind and the Willows* by Kenneth Grahame, illustrated by Ernest Shepherd, this edition published by Scribner's, 1954; p. 172 *A Tale of Two Cities* by Charles Dickens, illustrated by Richard Sharp, this edition published by Folio Society, 1954; p. 177 photo of Brontë by J. K. Rowling.

# Index

## A

Algonquin Round Table, 81
*Autobiography of Alice B.
    Toklas, The* (Stein), 61,
    69

## B

Baltimore Ravens, 27
Basket (Stein), 61, 66–68
Browning, Elizabeth Barrett,
    10–17, 76
    dogs and, 7, 11, 13,
        14–16, 17, 76
    as writer, 12, 13–14,
        16–17
Browning, Robert, 14–15,
    17, 76

## C

Catterina (Poe), 9, 24–25,
    26, 27
Charley (Steinbeck), 117–
    120
*Charlotte's Web* (White), 93,
    97–99
*Color Purple, The* (Walker),
    159, 163, 164, 167

## D

Dickens, Charles, 28–35,
    40, 172
    pet raven, 23–24, 29,
        33–34
    pets of, 7, 33–35
    as writer, 30–32, 34

## F

Faulkner, William, 45,
    88–91, 115
  dogs and, 90–91
  horses and, 7–8, 90, 91
  as writer, 90, 91
Flush (Browning), 13,
    14–16, 17, 76
*Flush: A Biography* (Woolf),
    17, 76

## G

Grip the Knowing
    (Dickens), 29, 33–34

## H

Harry Potter books, 169,
    171, 172–176
Hemingway, Ernest, 45, 66,
    91, 102–111, 115, 131
  cats and, 7, 103, 104–
    107, 108, 109–111
  as writer, 103, 105, 106,
    107–109

Henry, Marguerite, 122–125
  dogs and, 124
  horse of, 124–125
  as writer, 123, 124, 125

## M

Melville, Herman, 23,
    152–153
*Misty of Chincoteague*
    (Henry), 124–125

## N

Neruda, Pablo, 126–135
  life saved by dog, 7, 127,
    132
  pets of, 130, 131–133
  as writer, 127, 128,
    130–131, 133, 134–
    135

# O

O'Connor, Flannery, 140–
    147, 162
  birds and, 142–143
  illness, 146–147
  peafowl and, 8, 141, 142,
    144–146
  as writer, 141, 142,
    143–144, 146, 147

# P

Parker, Dorothy, 8–9, 78–87
  dogs and, 79, 80, 82–84,
    85–87
  as writer, 80–81, 84–85,
    86–87
pets, importance of, 6–8
Poe, Edgar Allan, 17, 18–27,
    124, 144
  cats and, 9, 19, 20,
    24–25, 26, 27
  as writer, 19, 21–24, 33
Potter, Beatrix, 50–59, 153,
    154, 156
  pets of, 52–53, 58
  as writer, 51, 53–57, 59

# R

"Raven, The" (Poe), 17, 22,
    24, 33
Rowling, J. K., 168–177
  pets of, 170–171, 174–
    175, 176–177
  as writer, 8, 169, 170,
    171, 172–176

# S

Sendak, Maurice, 7, 148–
    157
  dogs and, 151, 152,
    153–155, 157
  as writer, 149, 150–153,
    155–156
Shakespeare, William, 35, 54
six-toed cats, 109–111
Stein, Gertrude, 8, 60–69,
    106, 164
  dogs of, 61, 66–69
  as writer, 61, 63–65, 67,
    69
Steinbeck, John, 8, 112–121
  dogs and, 113, 114,
    117–120
  as writer, 113, 114,
    115–117, 118, 120–
    121

# T

*Tale of Peter Rabbit, The*
(Potter), 51, 55–56,
154
Toklas, Alice B., 63, 65, 66,
69
*Travels with Charley*
(Steinbeck), 113, 118–
119, 121
Twain, Mark, 36–45, 32, 99,
107, 138, 150
cats and, 7, 37, 38, 42–44
as writer, 38, 39–41, 44,
45

# V

Vonnegut, Kurt, 8–9,
136–139
dogs and, 137, 138–139
as writer, 137, 138, 139

# W

Walker, Alice, 158–167
chickens and, 8, 159, 160,
164–167
pets of, 164
as writer, 159, 160, 162,
163, 166–167
Wharton, Edith, 46–49
dogs and, 48–49
as writer, 48, 49
*Where the Wild Things Are*
(Sendak), 149, 152, 156
White, E. B., 8, 92–101
dogs and, 94, 96, 100,
101
pets of, 94
as writer, 93, 94, 95–96,
97–99, 101
Woolf, Virginia, 7, 17,
70–77, 162
dogs and, 71–73, 74–75,
76–77
as writer, 72, 73–74,
75–76

writing, about, 6–9